Richard Haynosz

Despite all we still have a soul

Contents

Part one

The most discernible order of the world

Part two

Part three

Part four

Existence is natural and obvious, but nothingness is only an abstraction, a notion created by a mind that – by its very presence – denies nothingness. However, existence as such is also an abstraction, because all that exists must do so in some definite mode. Reality has a specific construction – and if we want to understand it, we have to recognize it or at least imagine it. The work below presents a proposal for imagining reality, one that seems more impartial and probable than most others, including those commonly accepted.

Part one

The most discernible order of the world

1. Faith and confidence

If we want to maintain a reasonable distance to the world surrounding us and not fall into the snares of fanatical faith or the latest political religion, we should start to build a credible and rationally justified image of reality. One that, while being in accordance with our present knowledge, at the same time acknowledges the spiritual origin of the order of nature. This has been possible ever since modern science, and particularly cosmology, became an involuntary, but natural ally of religion, understood as a comprehensive grasp of reality. Recent studies clearly suggest that behind the cause of order in the world there must be some kind of intelligent complementation of matter: "Ultimate Reference", "Highest Intelligence", or simply – God. Purely materialistic explanations of the mechanism of the universe are no longer sufficient – all of them have ceased to be synonymous with science and progress.

Only a rationally-justified conviction about the existence of some higher intelligent force can offer a foundation for a new renaissance and let us endure the present confusion. I am not thinking here about a new religion, but rather about a rational complementation to the presently existing ones. There is a need for a common-sense concept providing a new, more intellectual-than-emotional, and logically-justified description of reality. We need an objective, unprejudiced picture that will liberate us from fanatical atheism and the resultant nihilism, give us back our status as partners in the construction of a more authentic and spiritual world, and provide hope for a future life.

But are we ready to surrender our unlimited personal freedom as offered by an empty heaven, along with the belief that our shrewdness gives us the right to take a place formerly reserved for God? Are we really interested in again becoming an important, responsible element of a greater whole and undertake the ensuing obligations?

I think we are, because we are just starting to understand that freedom reduced to a lack of obligations and limitations is only a harmful illusion, leading toward its opposition – the status of impersonal human resources that can be bought and thrown away after use. However, understanding alone cannot replace the idea of how to solve the problem. Remembering that all previous revolutions brought only suffering and disappointment, we must rely more on cold, sober reasoning than on emotions and superficial judgments. But this requires a return to the harmony between the spiritual and material spheres of reality. And first of all a solid, free-from-revelation justification of the Absolute as a truly existing and indispensable element of reality. Unfortunately, the last sixty years have proved that we cannot expect this from the Church – and even less from philosophy.

I realize that this demands time and effort. But there certainly are people who would like to work towards this end. I think about those for whom the purely material world seems incomplete and deprived of meaning, but for whom the belief that certain persons experience revelations and receive information straight from heaven is unacceptable. Nonetheless, they are still looking for arguments that may confirm their intuitive certainty about the rationality of the world. My aim is not to break with tradition, dogma, and rituals – but to justify them as symbolic reflection of the spiritual-material character of reality.

The text below offers a proposal for a model of reality that is in accordance with these presumptions. It does not contain any allusions to mysteries known only to me or to other persons, but can be easily understood by every literate reader. This model is also in agreement with Christianity, but mainly to the extent that it affirms the presence of an Ultimate Being, the existence of the human soul, and the possibility for its future continuation.

This work has been written independently, without affiliation with any religious group or other similar organization. It has been written in contemporary language and uses popular, scientific notions well known to the average, educated individual. None of the arguments presented here are based on mystical experiences, whether my own, or those of others.

Cognizance of God is beyond our ability, but the search for Him arises from the natural inclination of our mind as a part of our nature. We are drawn by three motives:

1. First is the internal need to relate our transient life to some kind of ultimate reference; to something that lasts eternally and is independently from us. This feeling need is supported by an intuitive certainty that such a reference really exists.

2. Second is the natural desire of the mind that recognizes the natural order of the world and feels the imperative to search for its cause.

3. Third is the irresistible longing to find in this order our own place and the aim of our existence.

The natural response to such tendencies was the creation of legends founded on historical events as well as on imagination, ones which became a justification for the way of thinking, customs and morality. The character and beauty of such legends was determined by the talents and degree of commitment of the given community. In the case of the prevailing and most popular religions they were always correlated with higher celestial forces personally interested in the fate of followers – the divine realm was closely connected with the everyday human world. This kind of faith was – and still is – justified and beneficial, but only in its historical times, that is until it falls in conflict with actual reality and in disagreement with spiritual development and with the harmony between human works and nature. This is a clear sign of the need to think about reforms or even the total change of credo.

In Europe the *Christian Legend* was widespread and officially obligatory roughly till the end of the First World War. After that it became open to changes of principles and to growing atheism. The laicization of culture is still proceeding and nowadays does so faster and more deeply than ever before. However, the more than 1500 years of deep devotion of the participants and the intellectual and factual domination as well as sincere involvement of millions of the most gifted minds – philosophers, scientists, talented artists, honest authentic craftsmen, and all others – contributed to the extraordinary attractiveness of this culture and virtually provided a Christian character to the rest of the world. The

Christian view of marriage, morals, ethics, freedom, families, etc. has proven to provide the best foundation for any civilization. The fact that Christianity was the first religion that spawned great centers of learning, hospitals, and churches is simply the outward, visible consequence of an internal phenomena: the miraculous change of the human heart in millions of individuals.

There are two ways in which the human mind responds in order to satisfy its intrinsic predispositions. The first one relies on faith in revelations – that is, on descriptions of the personal contacts of selected people with divine personages, and the second on the search for a logically justified explanation of the world. Throughout a prevailing part of history revelations were considered the foundation of faith; even now they comprise the essential element of many religions. The individual search for one's own truths has been – in most cases – limited either to commentary on official doctrine, or to a protest against it – that is, ultimately, to atheism.

However, along with the progress of science and the changing character of given civilizations, revelations have become ineffective as explanations of the order of nature. To believe in them now requires more confidence than the modern mind can afford. Most of us today see them as the literary enrichments of the mythical history of a given nation and are looking for the true nature of reality in science and life's experience.

But this path is still rather narrow and requires careful imagination as well as logical thinking and watchful observation of the surrounding world. It is still too early to expect a fully truthful picture supported by objective evidence, but it is certainly possible to construct one that is more probable than others.

This does not mean, however, that materialism is right! The official scientific hypothesis of spontaneous development "from parts to entirety" and "from lifeless to alive" is so contrary to experience that it requires a stronger faith than do the religions we so easily abandoned. At the same time, the progress of science and growing knowledge of nature clearly suggest that the order of the world is intentional. And this clearly points to the presence of an intelligence responsible for this intentionality. Even simple, everyday observation tells us that matter is only a passive substance unable to create on its own initiative any orderly and purposeful forms; and even less, those that are thinking and receptive. Only an external, intelligent creative force could give the world purposefulness and organization. Decisions always pass on from thought (that is, from spirit) to matter, never the reverse. In biology, from information contained in genes to the body; in politics and economy, from ideas to their implementation, in art and technology, from a theoretical model conceived in the mind of a designer to a finished work. The presentation of materialism as "the only scientific opinion" is contrary to practice and evidently false. Even the most superficial observation of the world shows that instructions are always transferred "from top to bottom", from ideas to matter, from concept to its realization, from thinking to thoughtless and from living to lifeless.

This hierarchy so visible in everyday life repeats itself on the scale of the entire universe. The presence of the spiritual, creative force reveals itself only indirectly by the logic of development and the purposeful organization of the surrounding reality. This simple analogy leads to the conclusion that behind the visible order of the world must be hidden something or someone who has shown enough intellect and motivation to conceive and execute this. Someone who is not only an abstract intelligence but also an individual person acting on the universal scale. Ultimately, then, we find in science the same information as in revelation – in their true essence both of them confirm the same most fundamental conclusion: the world has a dual, spiritual-material nature.

But this calls for more abstract thinking because instead of a well-known, caring guardian who created us in his likeness, we receive the unimaginable conceptual fusion of an intelligence with a permanent, active, immanent component of reality. In this case, intellect and motivation have been used for the same purpose – that is, for the invention and materialization of formerly invented ideas. Only we - all of us possessing a soul – may take a part in it in proportion to our fleeting life and primitive mind. And even such a modest share elevates our status. Once we stop believing that we are only purely material, unintended side effects of evolution, will we become individual, active participants in the cosmic plan and bear a proportional responsibility. Our mistakes and negligence hereafter affect not only ourselves, but the fate of the whole planet – and perhaps on the rest of the universe

We must then recognize several elementary facts. First, if (as physicists claim) the universe had its beginning, it must have happened in accordance with the principle that thought always precedes action. Since cosmology presumes that the whole universe is ruled by the same principles of logic, and by the same physical laws, there is no reason why only the universe should be the result of some incredible accident, not the outcome of a certain concept realized in an already-existing spiritual-material reality.

Second, our present knowledge of nature does not entitle us to claim that matter alone, drawn by some could create such a logically working entirety. Since there are no miracles on our level, they certainly do not happen on the universal level. If here on Earth buildings do not erect themselves, and gnomes do not come out from under the cupboard to fulfill our wishes, there is no reason why it could happen on the cosmic scale. Experience in the human world indicates that an idea always precedes its fulfillment. Therefore, there is no reason to think that this mechanism is completely reversed on the universal scale. The truth that the human order coexists with the natural one testifies that both belong to the same orderly universe.

It is true that modern science draws the conclusion about the rational functioning of the mechanism of the world from examination of matter, but this does not mean that this rationality must be accidental and aimless. Scientific methods simply cannot define this aim. A similar problem faces religion, which claims that the world is purposeful because it has been created by a rational God; although religion does not clearly describe what this purpose could be. So, despite the fact that these methods acknowledge the rationality of the world, both are equally helpless in drawing final conclusions. However, modern physics starts to confirm our intuitional conviction that there is no fundamental contradiction between faith and science.

The old argument that science can explain certain phenomena which, in years past, were seen as supernatural, is no longer a proof for the truthfulness of materialism. This old argument is nonetheless still used as a tool of manipulation and a kind of "secular opium for masses", mainly because both sides of today's "cultures wars" limit themselves to the easiest and most banal arguments. The massive retreat from religion does not stem from deep analysis, but rather from uncritical faith in the same, often-repeated superficial arguments.

The time has come to justify our intuitive conviction that the appearance and development of the universe resulted from a rational concept conceived by a higher mind. It is on this foundation that certain non-relative moral code must be defined. Although the question about the existence of God is more emotional than intellectual, the average person wants to be convinced that the presence of a higher mind is rationally demonstrated, and not in conflict with science. Science could not replace faith with its metaphysics, tradition, color, and ceremonies, but it can help to create a common foundation in the form of widely-accepted theism and commonly-observed morality. This will let us close our eyes to irrelevant details and open them to real values that go together with such conviction.

Faith based on the "Holy Scriptures" (of any religion) in its true essence means nothing more than strong belief in the words of other people – that is, in the words of consecutive authors and the commentators of a given text. The faithful person does not believe in the real God, but only in His image conceived by writers who claim to know how exactly He looks and what He wants (e.g., Moses who claimed to have met Him personally and have received the tablets with the Ten Commandments).

Confidence is closer to reality because it requires trust in words of the really living people who depend on the independent thinking of the person who tries to find truth by analyzing reality and looking for the most probable conclusions. Out of these two methods only confidence requires original mental effort and direct, independently collected knowledge. In the final account, all ways leading to God, including our own, are invented by human beings and are on a level of cognition much below certainty. But independently we are free to classify and select them in according with our intuition, experience, knowledge – as well as common sense and objectivity. Fortunately there are certain facts which make this possible. The most persuasive is the miracle of the simultaneous existence of conditions required to permit life on Earth, and the harmony visible between the earthly ecosphere and consecutive stages of cosmic evolution. These are phenomena that strongly support the opinion that a conscious intelligence is involved in its design and performance.

2. Reality

Materialism, as well as religion, are founded on the confidence that "somewhere out there" exists some kind of mysterious force responsible for the order of the universe. Materialists believe in an invisible "sub-reality", where the smallest particles of matter show the ability to start and self-sufficiently continue a purposeful process leading toward the construction of a rationally-organized world. Religious people believe in an indiscernible "over-reality" where lives a humanlike God who created a world designed, above all, for people. Both opinions are founded on the trust that there are some magical, external forces – either those that let the basic particles skillfully use the laws of physics to implement their goals; or superior beings (living in a higher, supernatural world) who are free from these laws. In both cases we are dealing with magical thinking and looking for explanations, either in consecutive lucky co-incidents or in mystical events.

Materialists have a hidden hope that this one, unusual exception to their dogma might be tolerated if it won't be called a miracle, but rather a "*singularity*" – an extremely rare condition in which no natural laws are any longer binding. In this case matter ceases to be dead and passive and starts to show intelligence and initiative in order to transform itself into a living organism. This would allow them to remain convinced that life evolved from matter. At the same time, creationists could maintain that these favorable conditions have appeared as an act of God's will in one miraculous act of creation. None of these can be verified, though each fits the given theory and allows its adherents to save face.

We will be certainly closer to the truth once we assume that there is only one reality, consisting of two, and only two, qualitatively different, but mutually complementing, elements: spirit and matter (that is, of conscience, thoughts, and emotions). In their pure form they are only ideas; but they become real and creative in mutual cooperation. Together they make the whole surrounding world - qualitatively complex, but spatially and functionally united. In this scheme, ideas do not make a separate, independent element of reality, but are only notions: the creation of intelligent minds; and, as such, belong to the realm of the spirit.

Consequently, all that exists consists of two elements only. Reality, thus comprehended, is universal and all-encompassing. It is not divided into homogenous, qualitatively-separate realms (exclusively spiritual or material), but composed of an endless number of particular beings, each of them consisting of these two elements in various proportions. The function and character of particular beings (and their position on the evolutionary ladder) results from the individual combination of these two elements. The share of lifeless beings in the spiritual sphere (thus their impact on reality) is limited to transfer a content which has been endowed to them by thinking and emotionally-capable living beings (e.g., books, pictures, mathematical equation, etc.).

In this reality eternally-existing matter (or energy) is an equivalent of eternally-existing spirit; and the reverse – eternally-existing spirit is an equivalent of eternally-existing matter (or energy). Together, they make the entire reality, and neither of them has a beginning or an end. That is why there is no need to look for a cause of their existence because it results from the very nature of being. They always simply *are* and together they make something *"that exists instead of nothing!"*. They create the constantly changing world, start and stop the flow of time, but unto themselves they are eternal and unchanging. And this ends the endless discussion about what was at the beginning.

This reality is the only one, and it is all-embracing and universal. There are no other, upper or lower realities restricted to initiated persons only. It includes all that exists between the highest form of spirit and the lowest form of matter, from the highest mind able to create original abstract ideas, to thinking and feeling living beings, and to things that are exclusively material. Its two basic components are equally good, and neither is corrupted or condemned in advance. This reality is organized according to unified physical and logical rules and fully cognizable in proportion to the mental and emotional (that is spiritual) advancement of the observer. If we cannot comprehend it entirely, it is because we perceive only the range of it to which we are actually entitled. There is no place here for creations of pure imagination, whether good or bad, such as spirits, devils, angels or any other phenomena of this kind.

It is quite obvious that any entirety (in this case, the universe) composed of a great number of qualitatively diversified spiritual-physical components that emerged under the influence of partially accidental circumstances must have two extreme forms: the highest and the lowest. On one side then should be the highest possible degree of spiritual-material harmony, and on the other, the simplest component of matter. I presume that the highest position is occupied by the most excellent mind, totally independent and unlimited in its thoughts and actions, which makes it an unavoidable condition for the existence of all rationally-organized reality, including the concept and performance of the existing universe. As a part of this complex reality, it is also, in a certain way, material, but without the necessity of constant passing away so characteristic for all others living beings. As its equivalent on the opposite, lowest side, there is the simplest form of matter (energy); which accepts only those forms that agree with the laws of physics and which intelligent beings wish to endow it with.

Summing up, we have on the one hand a living and dynamic force and on the other dead and passive matter of; all others are transitional and undergo modification the simplest kind. Both extreme forms are permanent and unchanging – all others are temporary and changing according to with the plan of universal evolution. Only two extremes appear in pure form – everything else (what exists), consist of these two elements represented in various proportions. In the active phase – that is, at creation and during the development of the universe – the amount of living, spiritual-material beings increases; while in the passive phase – between two consecutive universes – that amount is limited to only one, highest, single, and always-existing spirit, and to the most basic, dispersed, lifeless form of matter.

The division of reality into two different, but mutually-complementary forms - that is, spirit and matter - provides a foundation for the symmetry of the entire nature. It is present throughout it – in the ontological sense (chaos-order, action-stagnation, living-dead, lasting-passing away), as well as in the intellectual (good-evil, beautiful-ugly, truthful-false) and emotional sense (friendly-hostile, pleasant-painful, lovely-horrible). This symmetry of oppositions gives reality sense and meaning, creates space, and activates time.

3. Spirit and matter

By the term *matter* I mean nothing more than what physics considers as such. Simply stated, matter is a set of objects existing as substance (something that occupies space and has mass) or energy (ability to perform work). Matter is recognizable sensually and can be examined by scientific methods. Knowledge about it is commonly-accessible and taught in schools. By the *basic form of matter* I mean such a form that exists as (as physics claims) the ultimate, most simple component of all other forms. It has not yet been discovered, but the state of research is promising. Perhaps, regardless of the size, each sub-atomic particle is still comprised of yet smaller particles. Such an infinity would suggest that material equivalent of the Highest Intelligence also has potential for infinitive grow along with new experiences in creation of the next universes.

The notion of a "*spirit*" (or "*spirituality*") is considerably less precise and requires broader explanation. In this text, by the term "spirit" I mean the intellectual and emotional equivalent of matter, the everlasting component of the entire, all-comprising spiritual-material reality. A set (or rather a composition) of potential, immaterial psycho-intellectual attributes, consisting of the awareness of one's own individual distinctness combined with the capability to think and to feel emotions. In its pure form spirit is only an idea. To become real it must be associated with a living, individual organism. Then it becomes a *soul, a specific kind of spiritual entity* that can exist only individually in concrete, distinct, and separate form.

The genuine presence of the spirit begins with life. It separates all that is passive, thoughtless, and dumb from all that is active, thinking, and able to feel emotion. It also separates all that is totally dependent on the laws of physics from that which has a certain range of autonomy. Life is the first condition of participation (by a given being) in the spiritual sphere of reality. The spirit permeates the whole sphere of life from its highest to the lowest level – from the Absolute to plants - and reveals itself in direct proportion to the degree of freedom and intelligence.

Spiritual attributes are immaterial in the sense that they do not have such physical characteristics as dimensions, mass or energy and do not occupy space. They start to be real (that is, the results of their activity become verifiable) only in association with a definite, currently-existing living organism. The range of independence and rationality of a given living being remains in direct proportion to the degree of its spirituality, and grows along with its position on the ladder of evolution. Initially minimal, in its advanced form it creates a new, partially-independent-from-the-body, psycho intellectual unit called the soul. The presence of the spiritual sphere of reality is obvious and experienced in our daily life. Its existence contradicts the materialists' claim that at the bottom of the evolutionary ladder is matter alone.

Matter has never been observed to produce life, much less the non-material entity that is the human soul! The qualitative leap between these two phenomena is too big to be filled by an accident. While life as we know it involves matter, it does not derive from it by any natural way. Life is nothing short of a miracle conceived by an "*eternally-existing immaterial mind*".

We receive, then, the following chain of mutual dependences: there are no thoughts and emotions without a soul, no soul without a mind, no mind without a brain, no brain without a body, no bod y without life, and no life without matter. Material components depend on spiritual, and the reverse – spiritual on material. Life is, in its deepest essence, immaterial, but depends on proper physical conditions that could appear only in result of a process that was designed by the previous activity of thought and will. This dependence is common, all-embracing, and always binding. The best example of this could be the civilization we have created.

However, the fact that only materialized ideas become real does not confirm the identity of spirit and matter. It merely testifies to the existence of a mechanism that makes this codependence possible. There is no proof for the existence of physical laws which could compel matter to produce consciousness and invent ideas. Growth of complexity alone is not enough. Common experience points towards the reverse sequence: what is spiritual preconditions the emergence of what is material, and what is subjective preconditions the emergence of what is objective. All sensibly organized material forms may emerge only as a result of the previous initiative of thinking minds. Even everyday language indicates that thoughts and intentions expressed subjectively and described in the first person are a cause of the appearance of material things that are described in the third person (I have planted this tree). Initiative clearly goes from up to down, from living, thinking, and active to lifeless, thoughtless, and passive.

There is not even a single piece of evidence that dead, passive, and thoughtless matter was able independently, and without involvement of a living beings begin evolution, during which also accidentally-acting laws of nature could initiate consequent and directional development. Nor is there an explanation for why basic particles, deprived of inventiveness and initiative, could transform themselves into living and purposefully acting beings. Only the association of life with conscious mind, free will, and motivation – that is, with the soul – can create something new and provide meaning to matter! A child building a castle of sand is more creative than all the lifeless matter of the entire universe. intellect, create beings of quite opposite character. The very notion of *matter* describes a passive substance subject to physical laws.

It is true that are certain situations when physical cravings influence human will – this vital component of the soul – and change its natural behavior. Even non-addictive conditions like hunger or thirst can modify the actions of people. The soul is losing its normal dominance over the body, under the burden of unusual situations or mental disorder. This extraordinary event happens only when mutual cooperation between spirit and matter goes awry, e.g., by unhappy circumstances as when there is a lack of required harmony between these two elements.

Matter is present everywhere, either alone or in unity with spirit, in various forms, alive and lifeless, visible and invisible (e.g., electromagnetic waves), and behaves in accordance with physical laws acting in one or another given condition. Yet the spirit (consciousness, thoughts and emotions) as an immaterial quality of living beings must be linked to a specific living body residing in a particular place. Psychophysical entirety emerges only as a result of the unification of a particular composition of matter with a corresponding composition of spirit. Passive cannot, by itself, "generate" an active. Spirit is not an impersonal being that spontaneously unites with matter wherever it is ready for it. This means there must be some additional factor that makes it possible.

The first condition of the emergence of the spirit is the appearance of life. But life as such does not exist - it is also an immaterial, and therefore spiritual, attribute of a certain body. There is clear mutual dependence – there is no life without spirit and no spirit without life. However, the spirit, as the active component (of the spiritual-material reality), does not subordinate its existence to the accidental appearance of a particular composition of passive matter. There must be some other, notably external, reason. Let us start from the assumption that spirit is "sent from outside" to a particular body at the moment when this body reaches an adequate degree and kind of complexity. If this is indeed true, then we are dealing with the transmission of spirituality from some external source.

But what can this source be? According to Christian doctrine it is God who personally creates each individual soul. How would it be possible in a reality in which the spirit cannot exist independently, without being connected to a particular living body? The Gospel says (Luke 16:19-30) that a person's spirit can exist independent of his body though this is only temporary.

Perhaps, then, it is not a soul that has been created separately and later sent out to a specific body, but only an impulse that activates the abilities of matter; first to commence life and next for the creation and development of the soul? Perhaps we are dealing here with an analogy of photosynthesis in which, as the equivalent of light, is some kind of omnipresent intelligence that begins in the Absolute's mind, and is transferred to the body together with life? This would mean that the body does not receive a soul (from an external source), but only a stimulus starting its natural development in accordance with the laws of physics!

Such ab explanation has several advantages. It is easy to comprehend, it assures harmony between soul and body, it allows for the possession of a free will and for later independent growth. Finally, it liberates us from the embarrassing image of a massive (billions in the scale of the universe) "production of souls" in some kind of divine factory. Moreover, it refers to the first appearance of the soul in this life only, because all later reincarnations concern only the future phases of development of already-existing individuality.

I would like to add here three remarks. First, this explanation is far from materialism because it includes the presence of the Absolute and the existence of the individual soul as a separate being. Second, it refers exclusively to the higher forms of life that have the prospect of further growth by way of reincarnation. And third, this explanation is only an assumption, not a description, of the existing state – an illustration of the possibility of cooperation between spirit and matter that is in agreement with common sense; and could be placed within the realm of natural laws. Summing it up we can risk the following definition:

The "spiritual" is all that which does not have attributes of matter, but in cooperation with it generates real, verifiable results. The most obvious example is the materialization of ideas created by the minds of living beings

4. Life

Life is an attribute of a living organism, but in its true essence it is a spiritual phenomenon, not a physical object. Life does not have mass and dimensions, does not occupy space, create gravitation, or have any other physical characteristics. But despite this, it undoubtedly exists. Life becomes real only in connection with a body, not as just one of its many functions, but as the principal reason for its existence. It entirely depends on cooperation with matter, but has its own external origin.

Being the common attribute of many living organisms, it acquires endless forms, but still remains the same phenomenon. It appears only in specially-suited environments as an immaterial characteristic of a specific composition of matter. It is an indispensable condition for the realization of all remaining spiritual attributes, and therefore of the individual human person.

Each life – with the exception of the Absolute's – is temporary. This is the simple consequence of the fact that all that exists remains in eternal movement resulting in activation of the flow of time. This rule obligates in all scales of magnitude starting from the cyclical appearing and disappearing of consecutive universes thru particular planets down to their civilizations and to every living beings. But its end is not always the same and ultimate for every living species. I presume that homo sapiens, being the first who possess a soul, is also the first who has a chance to begin the long course of consecutive reincarnations preserving his/her personality till the end of the universe. This possibility is open for all those who will prove their ability for spiritual growth. This means that in the order of nature proposed here, the kind of death we undergo depends on our ability to use free will. It sounds exclusive, but this is a spiritual aristocracy, achieved by one's own effort and personal merits.

Let us now imagine a planet in the universe chosen for the performance of a drama and comedy of life. The stage is arranged with a master stroke, and action, although initially slow, gradually speeds up. Hot and dry rocks begin to be covered by plants, rivers start to flow, lakes fill with clean water and fish, and an entire, complicated system of living nature begins to function and becomes more and more beautiful. What a joy for the artist! Then come first signs of an intelligence, and finally, the first human beings with their potential soul. Even if they initially are not very sophisticated, at least one can look at them with some interest. For the first step has been made – the beginning of a certain independence from an accident and from direct influence of laws of physic, sufficient to change living beings into self-governing objects possessing a mind, emotions, free will, and ability to act. These creatures have many talents but do not know where they came from, why they are here and what part they are supposed to play! Or whether they have been employed permanently or for this one act only. Nevertheless, despite all the mistakes they still make some progress! And this gives them hope for participation in the next scenes of such a promising cosmic spectacle.

Transition from a dead object to a living subject marks the border between *"to be or not to be"*. Together with life we become aware about our own existence and of the rest of the world, as well as about our internal motivation and freedom to think and act. This allows us to exist as individuals and get a chance to participate in the universal enterprise of the development of the universe. This is certainly much more interesting than strictly planned creation!

Our own presence, as well as that of other similarly-thinking and feeling persons makes the universe emerge from nothingness and become authentic and real. Before the appearance of life the world was real only to its creator, the only existing mind. Now we can also take a part in the world's existence as an incomparably smaller, but spiritual and physical counterpart of its creator.

5. The Absolute

Since reality is only one and includes all that exists, this means that it includes the whole universe together with the cause of its appearance. If this cause means the active participation of motivated intelligence, it must also be a part of the reality described above and be united with some adequate kind of matter (energy).

But here arise questions resulting from the necessary coexistence of certain features which never occur together. How can one be a separate, individual person and at the same time an omnipresent element of the whole universal reality and interfere in the fate of all other intelligent beings? To occupy a distinctive space and have clear physical boundaries, but be involved not only intellectually but also physically in affairs of the whole huge universe, and supervise the course of evolution? Moreover, to combine these qualifications with features of a superior law of nature, which coordinates all others physical laws? And in addition, how can one possess the highest intellect, most sincere feelings, and the noblest motivation? Understanding such a complex being definitely transcends our imagination. So, to imagine it as a human being would be an obvious logical mistake, because there is no analogy between things known and unknown.

The question becomes a bit easier if we assume that the universe is not a strictly ruled entirety, but a collection of elements having a significant degree of autonomy and submitted to limited chance. Even if the direction of events has been decided by a previously designed course of evolution there is no reason why the author of the enterprise may want to be present everywhere and control everything personally. Nature is governed by its own principles and intelligent beings are responsible for their deeds and do not require constant supervision. Moreover, their spiritual growth must proceed independently because the possession of a soul gives them freedom and obligates them with responsibility. The universe is not a police state where everyone is suspected and closely observed! Perhaps in exceptional cases a certain kind of external intervention is desired (e.g., when there is a need to save a particular civilization or the whole planet), but this is rather the exception that confirms the rule. But although the highest creative force is at the same time the ultimate reference of values does not change the fact that it exists. And our duty is to imagine it, to name it, and (within our possibilities) to try to define it.

Let me start from the name. I do not want to use here the traditional name "God", firstly, because in monotheistic creeds, god is understood as someone who lives permanently in another, higher, purely spiritual reality – and secondly,

I would like to avoid any possible association with a variety of gods and their images presented by various religions. To prevent any possible misunderstandings I am choosing the historically justified and emotionally neutral term: "the Absolute". It is not very handy, but considering my approach to the subject, I definitely prefer to suggest an association with Platonic philosophy rather than with any presently existing religions.

Going a step further, everything that has a name should have a definition – if not of the thing itself, then at least of its image. It is true that the Absolute has never given His name or an explanation about the purpose of universe's existence. He wants us to figure it out by ourselves from observation of the nature of things. It is also true that accurate knowledge of the Absolute will always exceed the abilities of the human mind. But I know well that as long as we cannot define a being whose existence we want to prove, we cannot claim that such a being exists. All that is left to us is to hope that its character is reflected in the character of the world it has created. I realize that the impossibility of knowing the truth reduces this image to a foggy outline only. But even this may provide a starting point for a further dispute. I propose the following, very broad definition:

"The Absolute is the ultimate and most perfect of all possible incarnations of the idea of life and soul, an unification of the highest form of spirit with the highest form of matter. As the sole, necessary, and natural component of all-inclusive spiritual-material reality, He is eternal and independent from constantly changing external circumstances. His presence is as obvious and natural as

the existence of something instead of nothing. Thus, there is no need to search for the reason of His presence, in the same way as there is no need for such a search in reference to matter and physical laws.

As the most spiritual being, He unifies consciousness, the highest intellect, and the most noble emotions with the will to act and the possibility to rule over matter. Being the sole creator of original ideas, He is the indispensable condition for the existence of life and of all remaining spiritual attributes. As a consequence, He is also the author of the Grand Concept of the Universe in its changing form of constant, directional development, progressing from simple to complex, from lifelessness to living, and from thoughtless to thinking. He is also the author of all other former and future universes, whenever and wherever they may exist. As their creator He is actively and benevolently involved in the history of His creation.

He is also the sole, everlasting, rational being in the constantly changing reality. All other sensible and rational beings that have ever existed, do exist, and will exist are only transient, direct or indirect interpretation of His concepts. While undergoing cyclical changes along with His creation, He always remains the same, self-conscious individual person.

Comments

a. Life. Because all living beings emerge as a result of the unification of spirit and matter, then the authentically and eternally living Absolute must also fulfill the same conditions – that is, to be in some way material. This is a simple consequence of belonging to the same common reality. The principle that there is no soul without a mind, no mind without a body, no body without life, and no life without matter, also refers to the Absolute. Therefore He cannot be "above" reality, being a part of it as one of its two eternally existing components, which was not created by Him but had always been present as a basic condition of existence as such.

However, this contains a hidden contradiction, because life (as everything else) is always changeable and temporary; while the Absolute, to be eternal, must be independent from the flow of time and from fluctuations of environment. But since the soul is a form of the body, the perfect soul of the Absolute must be united with the perfect body, one that is free from changes due to the flow of time. We do not know how this could happen; but, in this case, modern science is on our side once again. Since energy changes its form, but never disappears, it cannot be dismissed that there is a kind of life that makes use of this. Even science seriously discusses the production of stem cells which may replace the deteriorating parts of a living organism. All this means that solving "the contradiction of eternal life" is ceasing to be a fantasy, and is becoming a technological problem.

b. Presence and activity. If all that is spiritual must be material (at least to some degree) to become real, the same rule applies to the Absolute. However, as a spiritual-material and individual person, He must also be in a particular time and place. But how can these notions apply in reference to infinity and eternity? How can one be omnipresent and simultaneously occupy a clearly defined space with physical boundaries? Can these two opposite characteristics be compatible? At first glance this seems impossible; but let us remember that quantum physics proposes certain scientific explanations that seem to be equally controversial. I am not saying that miracles really happen, but can we be sure that that some kind of direct influence of thoughts on matter is, in all circumstances and on every level of development, totally excluded? Maybe there are some laws of nature which allow for it. Even physics, the apex of science, mentions the influence of the consciousness of the researcher on the results of some experiments.

We know that the Absolute does not reveal Himself personally, but by means of His activity. His presence reveals itself through the spiritual inspiration of exceptionally sensitive and talented individuals who contribute to the growth of civilization, or to the change of its direction. He can be found everywhere where the good, the true, and beautiful are visible in human works – in a new symphony, a wise law, or a successful medical operation. Using poetic language, we may say that the nature of the Absolute lets Him be present in these exact times and places. By guessing His immaterial thoughts and expressing them in matter we create a friendly and beautiful reality. We know from the depths of our hearts that "absolute values" make a natural part of the Highest Wisdom, this indispensable condition for successful universal evolution.

The presence of the Absolute is proportional to the degree of His engagement in the history of His works and is expressed by the current level of the order of a given part of the universe. He is everywhere that He creates and realizes His ideas. And this means that every currently existing universe, in its entirety as well as in chosen places, exemplifies the materialization of His thoughts. This also relates to intelligent beings, who, while cooperating with Him, adapt the quality of their surroundings to the current stage of their spiritual development. By analogy to human projects, we may assume that the Absolute, as an intellect and the designer of the universe, is somehow "outside" of the cosmic experiment; but as its active performer, He is also "inside" of it. This renders the question of whether God is inside or outside of the world quite irrelevant.

If the Absolute had not lowered Himself to the level of His creation He could not transfer His ideas into reality; He would remain in a state of ideal excellence and passive contemplation. Practically speaking, He would not exist, together with everything He has created, including anybody else who would be able to notice His presence._However, the fact that humans are incapable of comprehending or recognizing Him either directly or overtly does not mean that He is absent (or tantamount to nothingness), but only that He is beyond our unmistakable cognition. The existence of higher beings is not dependent on the existence or recognition of lower ones.

c. Existence. The existence of the Absolute is clearly confirmed by the steady progress of the order of the universe. Scientific confirmation of directed cosmic evolution provides reasons to search for its cause. The fact that it is a "way of existence" of the universe implies that it is intentional rather than accidental. If this was the only, single proof for His existence, it would be still much more than the lack of any evidence for His non-existence. The fact that this is in accord with our hopes and intuition does not make it any less likely, as it results from rational thinking; and it would be the same even if we were not capable of any emotions.

It is true that the majority of people are looking for the presence of the Absolute personally – intuitively and emotionally. And visions, revelations and mystical experiences provide the foundations for many religions. Cast into this cold and indifferent universe we need someone who understands its mechanism and who is able and (more importantly) is willing to help us. We therefore create our own, subjective picture of the Absolute adapted to our needs and to the range of our comprehension; and we put Him in another, higher reality – even though such a reality does not exist. This does not, however, change the fact that the Absolute simply, really, and objectively exists as a necessary condition for the rationality of the world.

All mystical experiences indicating the existence of "another world" remain purely subjective and thereby unverifiable (even if some people truly experience them). Indeed, when judged according to contemporary criteria they are completely improbable. Thus, regardless of their meaning in the history of religion and civilization, we must classify them as "*subjective truths*", which, as a concept, is internally contradictory and does not fit within the premises adopted here.

d. Comparison. If we were able to recognize and fully understand the Absolute, it would mean that He is barely an improved, more powerful human. And this would decidedly be insufficient to create such a complex and magnificent *magnum opus* as the universe. Yet, while accepting all possible differences, we have to remember that He, as well as we, belong to the same spiritual-material reality. If so, we must have certain common features. Not of the same quality, but of the same kind. The most obvious are life, consciousness, intellect, initiative, motivation, and the ability to act and to feel emotions. This suggests a comparable way of thinking. If the Absolute was using quite different logic, He could not create a world in which we were able to survive and develop to the present level. The fact that the world can be comprehended by a rationally-thinking human mind testifies that, despite all the differences dividing us (that is human beings and the Absolute), we both are individual persons possessing souls. And this certainly excludes the concept of "thinking matter", because matter, by definition, is lifeless and unaware of its own existence.

e. The lowest and the highest. The spiritual development of living organisms increases along with the growth of complexity, but it does not proceed proportionally. On the higher stages of development, the spiritual changes are greater than the physical. (For example, the genetic code of primates differs from human's only about 1%, while with one species we see great civilizations, and with the other merely simple survival). Since this principle obligates below the human level, there is a justified possibility that it also obligates above it. Since there is no reason to think that we are the highest possible intelligence on the scale of the entire universe, we have to assume that universal reality contains a hierarchy of more spiritually advanced beings. I am not talking here about angels or other semi-divine figures, but about the inhabitants of other planets who are actually on different levels of spiritual advancement. If this is so, then they must be accompanied by more and more excellent, but to some degree similar, bodies. We do not know how many steps lead toward the unification of the highest spirituality with the most excellent body, but there must be many of them; and every next one is going to be a bit better that the former.

f. Probability. It is true that the definition of the Absolute given above is highly speculative, and that He will forever remain unimaginable and beyond any experience. But it is also true that the picture of an exclusively material, but fully-coherent world is much less probable and in conflict with observation, common sense, and intuition. Because we cannot resist the internal conviction about His presence, we feel an irresistible need to build His most feasible image. In most cases, it is made on the pattern of the human beings because all others would be totally non-understandable and therefore too horrifying to accept. To be understood an image of a higher personality must be adapted to the level of comprehension of lower minds, and in most cases the final result is still far from perfect and full of controversies. The only way out is to consent with those forms that seem to be relatively rational and acceptable, and to reject those that are clearly subjective or in conflict with the actual picture of the contemporary world.

g. Alternative. One may of course claim that the Absolute does not exist, and that only we, the people, are the sole intelligent observers of the spontaneously-emerged universe. But then the goal and meaning of such a universe would be reduced merely to what we are able to provide it with. And this, considering our limited intelligence and egoism, selfishness, and cruelty would be decisively not enough to justify such a great enterprise. Moreover, we do not know enough facts to guess the exact meaning of something that not only precedes our presence here, but also makes it possible. The result cannot be its own cause. If the universe were meaningless, this would refer to our thoughts about it, as well. The level of rationality of the human mind reflects the rationality of the world. By negating the rationality of a cause we undermine the rationality of result. Only being a logical part of a greater whole can justify the consistency of our thinking. This dependency works only one way and is never reversible, because it stems from the very essence of the order of universe. Therefore, it is always binding; no matter if our presence here is intentional or only accidental.

h. Cause and result. An exclusively-material universe does not explain itself without relation to something that exists apart and independent of it. It acquires meaning only as part of a cosmological system which has its source in some intelligent, creative force. But if this force were external in relation to the universe, we would be forced to look for the cause of its existence; next for the cause of the cause, and so on, without end. However, if the cause and its result make natural and eternal components of the same, single reality, and create the mutually-complementing entirety, then the centuries-long discussion about reason and sequence rationality of the human mind reflects the rationality of the universe. The negation of the rationality of the cause is tantamount to the negation of the rationality of its results. Only being a logical part of a greater, rational entirety of the above components' appearance loses its significance. The Absolute is the creator, but at the same time an inevitable, natural part of this all embracing reality, and simultaneously one of the reasons for its existence.

1. Extent. Since in this model of the world the Absolute makes an unavoidable condition of existence for all rational things, the question arises whether He is also the creator of the laws of physics. Or are they intrinsic traits of matter (its natural attribute), resulting from the very fact of its existence? And as such, they are eternal and obligatory in this and every other universe, wherever and whenever existing. In this case they must come from the permanent principles of logic and mathematics that are an intrinsic feature of the Highest Mind and, to a certain degree, of every other intellect. This means that both of these traits (that is, physical laws and principles of logic) exist independently of the presence of minds that may be able to recognize and apply them; including the mind of the Absolute who identifies with them as with His natural attributes.

2. This state of affairs remains in close agreement with the idea of the one, single reality. It also has some other logical justifications. At first, it provides a stable continuation of universal evolution as purposefully-planned technology leading to the intended result. The total supremacy of the Absolute over physical laws would collide with the further, consequent course of development of the universe, and make difficult the cooperation of intelligent beings. Since the Absolute, at the time of His creative activity, resigns from His perfection, He is not completely free from spontaneous decisions. If they involved the laws of nature, it could disturb the harmony of further development. To exclude such possibility, the Absolute would have to be subject to a set of external moral laws higher than Himself. And this is not in conflict with the model of one, all-embracing reality.

3. Steady behavior of matter in accordance with the laws of physics does not decrease intellectual freedom of the Absolute, but only forces Him to take into account existing conditions. But this are natural conditions connected with every creative work. At the same time, full knowledge of these laws gives Him an almost unlimited number of possible applications; including those which by human minds could be perceived as miracles. Lack of total freedom of choice does not influence the work of the Highest Mind, who still remains creator of all that is purposeful, beautiful, good, and beneficial.

Conclusion: The Absolute can be identified with eternally and universally binding, physical laws. This unity is one of His essential characteristics in the same way as is the code of elementary, undeniable moral values. He cannot alter them at will or adapt them to solve unexpected problems throughout the existence of the actual universe.

j. Emotions. The definition of the Absolute given above refers to His image in the purposeful and rationally-built universe. It does not contain information about His attitude toward living and intelligent beings. It does not say if He is indeed forgiving and caring or whether He loves, or merely tolerates them. We can only conclude that as "*the most perfect of all possible incarnations of the idea of life and soul*", He is the equally perfect embodiment of the good, the true, and the beautiful; and of the most sincere feelings and noble motivations. And hope that in being "*actively and benevolently involved in the history of His making*", He is looking at us with some good will, sympathy, and tolerance. But even if this is true, it does not mean that He intervenes in every single life and protects us from the effects of our mistakes. He rather expects that we by ourselves will comprehend the moral truths resulting from the nature of His creation, and fulfill the conditions required to complete His design. He expects our conscious cooperation in successfully building the best of all possible worlds. Our duty is to rise up to His expectations, cooperate with Him in this work, and to play our part.

But isn't God's love for people a foundation and condition of faith? Well, even if it is, His very existence does not depend on our beliefs. He has not emerged to become a consoler of humanity, but has existed always as an empirical fact, the necessary condition for the order of the world and our presence in it, independent from our opinion or our mutual love. Our faith or lack of it can change only our human world, but further development of our spirituality demands a creative balance between nature and intelligent beings on all stages of existence. The destruction of such harmony on a given planet means resignation from the already achieved level and the end of its development. And our present, selfish civilization has brought us dangerously close to this point

k. Contact. At the time of polytheism, contacts with divine persons were frequent, direct, and considered natural. The method was to gain the attention of a particular divinity by giving it an offering and asking for help. Pieces of practical advices were transmitted by revelations and magical signs, and perceived by trusted individuals – prophets, priests, and monarchs. The effectiveness of these petitions was evidenced by their success (or failure) in solving a given problem, e.g., conquering or defending one's territory. Faithfulness was awarded by victory and apostasy punished by calamity.

The same form of communication has been transferred to relations with a solitary god who was not merely one of many residents of Olympus, but one who has taken over all power and all duties, and with them the entire devotion of the faithful. Because the personal fate of believers was strongly related with tribal interest, monotheistic religions become even more closely connected, or even identified with state power (*cuius regio eius religio*). In effect, the state became interested in the faithfulness of its subjects. Serious doubts and apostasy were considered harmful for the community and severely punished, sometimes even by death. The first example of this was provided by Moses, who ordered 3,000 people to be killed for such an innocent activity as dancing around a Golden Calf. The same attitude can be seen in Islam, which commands to kill all those who want to leave the faith, (Koran 4:92). The exception to this is contemporary Christianity, which under the influence of secular civilization, separated itself from the state and became much more gentler and tolerant. It took almost two thousand years to draw such conclusion from the teachings of Jesus Christ.

But since the vulnerability of human beings and our need of help are still here, such a utilitarian attitude toward religion is still present. Nevertheless, in monotheism, where the distance between The Only God and His followers is significantly wider than in polytheism, contacts with the divinity acquired a different form. The human being can no longer count on such a direct, personal interest and attention as Pallas Athena felt toward Odysseus. It is no longer the friendly help shown by a well-known acquaintance, but rather mercy shown to a faithful subject by an omnipotent, but somewhat unpredictable, absolute ruler.

This situation changes when we step up to the next level of monotheism where the one and only God, so comparable to man, has been replaced by the distant Absolute. He does not do anything to be recognized or understand by humans. He doesn't tell them His name or try to show them how to behave in order to remain in agreement with the world. He wants them to guess the "rules of the game" by observation of reality and by use of their minds and intuition. And surprisingly we have succeeded enough to make significant progress.

We have finally started to understand that we shall never deny the possession of our own soul and resign from our share in making the world better in proportion to our possibilities – especially while doing this on behalf of some political or other egoistic ideology that so often leads to disaster. However, contact with the Absolute requires an intellectual and emotional conviction about presence of some Upper Order of the World and confidence in further life and development of our souls.

We can no longer count on offering this or another gift in exchange for support for their case. The difference between the two sides is too big. On the one hand there is a personage on the scale of the whole "universum" who needs nothing from us – and on the other, the merely fleeting problems of small ants with strong instincts and moderate intelligence. The only bond and similarity between us is possession of the same spiritual traits – life, intellect, and the ability to feel emotions.

This does not exclude, however, the possibility of contact. Rather the reverse: it makes it more probable because we and He live in the same, common reality where transcendence refers to the quality and level of spiritual development of living beings; but not to their kind. It gives us the possibility and hope to gain a short moment of His attention. I am not talking about revelation in the form of personal encounters, but about intellectual and emotional inspiration. However, since the Absolute never imposes His presence upon us, the initiative has to come from our side and be spontaneous, frank, and honest. Perhaps then may we overcome the distance that divides us from Him. If we can afford this, we may achieve a sudden influx of energy and optimism that might help us find a solution, regain courage, and overcome difficulties.

There are many ways leading to this. The easiest is to elevate our thoughts above the everyday fight for survival. More difficult is the conscious and active involvement in the betterment of the world; but the most demanding is the spontaneous attempt to overcome the distance dividing our souls. Then, perhaps, the Absolute will let us feel His presence for a moment.

1. Justice. The Absolute is, by His very nature, impartial, neutral, and truthful. Being an unavoidable condition of the universal order, He cannot be engaged in the fate of particular nations, take part in their quarrels with neighbors, or stay on one or another side. Cases of punishment or reward are regulated by the ever-present natural law. Hard-working and honest people are usually rewarded (by natural mechanism of the world), personally and commonly and therefore in their majority happier. Mainly because they are closer to the universal order than their lazy and corrupt counterparts.

In this scheme there is no place for the all-forgiving love of God for the whole of humanity. The notion of the redemption of the *entirety* of humanity (because of committed sins) becomes invalid. Redemption or condemnation could be expected only personally in the case of an individual, single life. There are two basic criteria – the ability to make even small personal progress and to leave the world a bit better than it would be without your participation.

The Absolute cannot be a "jealous God" because, as the indispensable component and condition of existence of organized reality, He does not have any competitors. He does not care whether we believe in Him or how we imagine Him because he knows that we have to do so in accordance with our experience and modest mental possibilities, and therefore our imagination of Him will be always imperfect. But even this is enough to acknowledge His presence and draw the proper intellectual and moral conclusions. Lack of imagination will be forgiven if we will show a basic decency, good will, and compassion toward others.

Awareness that morality is based on the essential structure of the world obligates us to be self-reliant and responsible - not only for ourselves, but for the fate of the whole planet. From this point of view, the Absolute begins to be less needed as a good father, merciful guardian, and consoler, and starts to be indispensable as the reason of existence. We are losing part of His personal care, love, and forgiveness, but we are gaining freedom and responsibility. Justice is expressed in principles of reincarnation that guarantee to all of us impartiality, understanding, and (for the majority of us) the chance for a future life. Everyone faces the same choice:

either you pass the practical examination of every consecutive life or dissolve your personality in the magnitude of the universe. There is no maturity without responsibility! But please notice that even this perspective is much better than the prospect of hell, and not a bit worse than what is promised by materialists.

m. Individualism. The appearance and life of an individual person possessing a soul is one of the goals for the existence of the universe. The destination of thinking beings is to become mature partners of the Absolute. Each individual can earn his or her personal *salvation* by decent behavior and good deeds, proper endeavor and by many other ways endorsing harmony between individuals and society or humanity with nature.

I would like to remind once more that we humans were never born in a sinful state or collectively condemned as a species for some legendary disobedience. The entirety of humanity has never been in a "lost" condition or in need of a savior.

Jesus Christ appeared as extraordinary envoy from the Absolute to help us to change the false course of Roman civilization from a ruthless fight for power to more gentle and friendly attitude toward others.

6. The soul

By the term "soul" I understand a truly existing and conscious of its own existence, autonomic unit of mutually-linked thoughts and emotions. The authenticity of the soul so defined is obvious and commonly acknowledged. The appearance of the human soul – as the realization of the universal idea of an intelligent creature adapted to earthly conditions – comes as a natural consequence of the general concept of the universe. Beings possessing a soul are not a by-product of natural selection, but the very aim itself. The lives of these persons are simultaneously going on in two separate, but mutually dependent realms – the spiritual and physical. This is not, however, an equal share because the soul always dominates the body as main source of motivation and decisions – at least in normal conditions. But there are of course circumstances when physical urges – like hunger, pain or danger – force the soul to surrender to the demands of the body. But this happens only when the soul has been deprived of free will, making it disabled and incomplete.

Acts of hearing, seeing, etc. are functions of the body. But self-awareness, consciousness, logic, the ability to invent, abstract thinking (understanding notions like freedom, truth or beauty etc.), imagination and ability to feel emotions (especially higher feelings like love, compassion etc.) are functions of an immaterial *mind* which belongs to the spiritual part of reality. We receive a *mind* potentially ready to develop, together with life. It is a separate entity, characteristic for humans or perhaps for other species with adequately complex bodies. The immaterial works only in close cooperation with corresponding functions – in this case with the *brain*. When we progress in life and collect experience and education, our mind acquires an individual personal character and becomes *"the earthly soul"* – a separate entity with the ability to develop and keep its own reserve of some kind of energy needed for transfer into another body.

The earthly soul being strictly individual and personal, responds positively to the mind of the Absolute, this eternal source of universal inspiration containing all possible ideas. It activates the abilities of the soul and makes possible changing these inspirations into true reality. The soul becomes real with the moment of integrating itself with a proper individual and living body, possessing adequate physical features – in our case the brain or its equivalent. Activation of the spirit may be compared to radio broadcasts which becomes useful everywhere where there exists suitable receiver used by a person who understands incoming messages. Process similar to developing civilization ready to produce intelligent personalities. This expresses the omnipresence of the Highest Intelligence filling the whole universe and activating itself everywhere that proper conditions exists.

Thanks to the possession of the earthly soul we can observe facts, draw logical conclusions, comprehend and create ideas, and give them material shape. The soul alone gives us freedom of choice and the possibility to use this gift for our own aims. This is possible thanks to such traits of the soul as conscience, reflection, free will, motivation, ability to act, responsibility, and other immaterial characteristics. The fully-developed soul is not a necessary condition for life which, at its lower stages, can very well manage without it.

The soul is not a sudden, unexpected phenomenon fitting and proper for humans only. It appears together with life and undergoes slow and systematic development. Along with successive stages of evolution we see the growing independence of living beings from direct influence of the laws of physics and the increasing share of individual decisions.

The marvel of the human soul relies on the sudden (on the time-scale of evolution) appearance of a complete intellectual-emotional unit, which to a significant degree dominates instinctive behavior. The qualitative difference and independence from the body became so great that this phenomenon not only deserves a separate classification, but also justifies hopes for its further existence as well as for self-sufficient and individual development.

I will be using here the notion "soul" in two meanings. The first relates to the truly existing human soul which I will call the "earthly" or the "active" soul. This term expresses the real, obvious presence of the human soul, without suggesting its possible further existence. The second notion suggests its possible continuation and development after the death of the body as the "heavenly soul". I shall start from a description of the first category. I propose the following definition of the "active soul":

The "earthly soul" is the autonomous, intellectual-emotional complex that combines awareness of its own separate existence and individuality with intellect motivated by emotions and emotions controlled and modified by intellect. In its true essence this unit is immaterial and realizes itself fully only in unity with the body.

In the course of the experiences of life it changes from a potential soul into an active soul and becomes fully real, able to comprehend universal ideas, to create new ones, and to give them a material form. Along with its development, it gains greater independence from the body and becomes

an active participant in the universal spiritual sphere. The "earthly soul" is a higher manifestation of life, a new quality that gives us freedom and determines our individuality.

When receiving life, we emerge from the darkness of nothingness and begin to see the world within a range accessible for our senses. But only the soul permits us to understand the world, gives us an awareness about our separateness from the rest of things, and opens before us the gates to a higher existence. Only through the soul can the world be perceived and interpreted, become interesting and acquire meaning. It starts to be made up of not only what had already existed when we opened our eyes for the first time, but also of what we have created and of our immaterial thoughts and feelings. Even possession of our present, still modest soul opens before us the beginning of a great spiritual world, with its further, endless possibilities. Development that begins so modestly can, in the broader perspective, become close to the perfect and solely original personality of the Absolute.

The appearance of the soul begins a completely new quality, the first spiritual element of a great eminence, absent in all former stages of evolution. This is also the first, in the history of Earth, and perhaps of the whole universe, individual personality conscious of its own separate existence, capable of overcoming the principal animalistic motivations. It is also the first intrusion into realms of abstract thinking, moral obligations, and artistic inspirations.

God gives everyone the right to possess a soul, but not to its further growth and continuation. However, He does not expect from us too much because He knows that we are still at the very beginning of the road, taking only the first step in the right direction. The future life is not given for free. We must fulfill the tasks we have been called for, respect the dignity and rights of other thinking individuals, and show benevolence and good will toward all living creatures. We must also show the ability for objective self-assessment of our own deeds in light of obligatory universal morality and readiness to bear personal responsibility. If you do not make personal progress or an effort to improve the world even a bit – do not anticipate that you will carry your soul over the threshold of death. The possession of a potential soul is an inherited privilege, but its transformation into an "active soul" requires an act of will.

7. Reincarnation

There is no doubt about the real presence of the "earthly soul". The sentence: "The earthly soul exists" is true. However, it raises the next intriguing question. Can this one, individual soul exists only in association with this one, particular and currently "possessed" body; or perhaps with some other, similar one? In other words, does the soul possess a body or rather the reverse – does the body possesses a soul? What is permanent and what is transient?

Taking into account the long and extremely complicated process leading to the emergence of this still-imperfect soul, ordinary constructive logic indicates the probability, and even necessity, of its further development. Wasting such a long preparation for such a miserable result would be an illogical exception in a rationally-organized reality. Therefore, the continuation of the existence and development of the soul seems much more likely than its complete disappearance. And this gives us encouragement to reflect over its possible course. Let us start from the obvious assumption that such an individual development will be no longer linked up with the advancement of the whole species, but with its single representatives. This means that the further existence of our soul will again depend on its connection with a particular, living, individual body. (Besides, the image early Christians had about the future fate of the human soul was not too far from the concept of reincarnation. St. Paul, in his letter to the Corinthians (15:50-53) says that what is mortal will inherit the immortal (the soul) and we all will be changed. *For what is perishable must put on the imperishable, and this mortal must put on immortality.* This is not an obvious description of reincarnation, but analogy is sufficiently clear.)

We know only too well how little can be achieved in the course of a single life, which so often comes to an end when we still have our full spiritual abilities. Seen from the perspective of youth, it seems to be endless and magnificent; but retrospectively, turns out to be short and unfulfilled. (307) Only the sum of all the thoughts, emotions, efforts, and sufferings that one can experience in consecutive reincarnations can elevate us to the height where we could fully comprehend the intentions of the Absolute, or come into some kind of contact with Him. Considering our present status, these expectations seem to be insolent and presumptuous – but bearing in mind what a long road opens before us, there is still a hope that someday a small group will attain the satisfactory qualifications.

From a purely practical point of view, the simplest way to the further enrichment of the human soul would be the repetition of the process of positive selection that had already proved so successful. That is, to give it the opportunity to experience challenges and difficulties anew, in many consecutive lives. Because only a diversity of experiences can assure the independence and uniqueness of each subsequent incarnation, they shall take place in a different environment – or even better, on different planets. It is not of course to be excluded that some individuals may get a chance to repeat their life once more here on Earth – but thinking constructively, this would be the exception rather than the rule. I imagine that the most likely course of events is as follows:

a. We are born with a soul which, in its initial form, is only potentially immortal; but has the ability to expand this potential.

b. Experiences of life and one's own effort can change such a potential soul into a complete, mature, spiritual entity – the "earthly" or "active soul". This outcome is open to everybody; but guaranteed to nobody.

c. If an individual person succeeds in making such a conscious, lifelong effort, the "earthly soul" becomes an individual, autonomous being, with a spiritual and energetic potential sufficient to survive the death of the body. Then, it is transferred to the next one to create a new, complete, psycho-physical entity. The same process will be repeated in each following life. The fleetingness and fragility of a single life is balanced by consecutive, ever more perfect incarnations. Thanks to them, the soul achieves a level where it changes into a permanent element of the universe, taking part in all successive phases of its future development.

d. Since every consecutive life is a test, there must be some obligatory, clearly articulated conditions to be met in order to pass them successfully. Speaking boldly, they are as follows: "Do not be an egoist, but rather demonstrate the will to make the world a bit better than it would be without our contribution. Cooperate with the Absolute and take an active part in the joint creation of the universe. Act like a medieval knight who deems himself a guardian of divine order and justice."

Unresponsiveness to the suffering of others and complete intellectual laziness also mean resignation from any further prospects. Basic decency and responsibility in everyday life is as obligatory as conscious, individual effort to accomplish the best possible results in whatever one is doing. It is not a question of great works or significant achievements – they count less than persistence, benevolence, and goodwill. The goal is *perfection of the individual who is reaching the maximum of what a human being – considering his nature – can achieve.* And to do so in accordance with natural law and common decency in relationships with nature and other people. Only personal responsibility gives us an admission ticket to the club of candidates to the better world.

e. This is the repetitive battle for participation in the game of life. We do not know how much more demanding each next incarnation will be in comparison with the former one, but each of them is a consecutive test that brings a gradual improvement of soul and body. However, independently of this, I am sure that we can always expect the

Absolute to show a tolerance for His "lesser brothers," and to give some of us a second chance to correct our mistakes. But to count on this could prove very risky. The final stage would be reached only by those who are able, in each consecutive life, to make personal progress – to leave life more mature than they were at the beginning of it. We do not have even the slightest grounds to know how many incarnations would be needed in order to achieve this ultimate purpose; but considering how little can be done in one single life, there will be many.

f. But if we fail several examinations, the worst we can expect is the dissolution of our individual soul in the great spirit of the cosmos. I definitely reject the existence of hell or any other place of this kind. The Absolute is righteous; but is not vengeful. Therefore He cannot expect too much from our small, freshly-formed souls. Apart from understandable moral reservations, the existence of hell as a place of constant suffering does not fit into the universal organization of the world as contrary to general harmony. The very existence of a place where millions suffer forever while some others enjoy an eternal happiness will destroy moral foundations of the universe. It will be fair enough if those who do not respond to the voice of conscience end their existence by ultimate disappearance. That is exactly how it has been promised by "secular progressives".

g. This kind of reincarnation differs fundamentally from what is understood by this term in other religions. It is much closer to the Christian, and particularly to the Protestant philosophy of activity and hard work leading to salvation than to the Eastern version with its emphasis on passivity, avoidance of temptation, and suffering. The aim of consecutive reincarnations is *not* to become free from desires and suffering in order to be finally, with a sigh of relief, dissolved into universal nothingness. Humanity is *not* helplessly thrown into the chaos of life by some unidentified external forces and life is *not* a punishment for the soul for its association with a "corrupt" body.

Quite the contrary – it is a reward! The soul and body still belong to different qualities; but constitute a harmonious unity and complete each other. Life is an exceptional gift from God, valuable in itself; a reason for constant joy and opportunity to act; something worth caring about and worth the effort of making it beautiful and useful. The goal is to live fully; not in indifferent passivity. The recurrent coming into being and passing away is *not* a hopeless spiral of sorry incidents that should be left behind as soon as possible, but the road leading to perfection.

h. Consecutive reincarnations will let us to take part in all levels of advancement of the universe and experience all that life may offer. They will bring wisdom and mastery in everything we do, and to influence the improvement of the universe. Moreover, these possibilities increase because each next life provides the opportunity to improve the body and soul. We will achieve the permitted perfection only after all that is possible is fulfilled and nothing is left that could still be desired. We will end our long journey with the confidence that we have seen all that could be seen and have lived through all that was worth living through. When we will be close to *the most perfect soul and most subtle body* in complete peace, we will join the universal soul of the Absolute. We will never become a pure spirit because all that is real must also, to some degree, be material. Neither will we disappear without a trace, because the experiences collected for millions of years will allow us to last forever as an individual input to all future universes. The essence of reincarnation is constant passing away and constant reappearance on a level higher than before. There is no chance to turn back on the ladder of development: for the choice is clear– either you make progress or disappear forever.

The fact that the world will never be perfect is not a reason to put our life into a framework of one's own, narrow egoism. The opposite is the case: risking one's own interest in defense of values and principles is what counts the most in the evaluation of this, and every next life. Our task is to bring our soul to its best and fully satisfying form. We are *not* involuntary victims of an accident, but individuals chosen to play an active part in the realization of the Great Cosmic Enterprise. Reward is participation in subsequent reincarnations, and satisfaction from work well done. This constant ascension will open before us new, endless horizons and give us a sense of victory.

The confidence in having a soul can be undoubtedly and logically defended without help from old texts or prophetic visions, but exclusively on the basis of sober reasoning. Similarly, there is not the slightest antagonism between spirit and matter. On the contrary, the beauty of the universe is founded on the perfect, mutual cooperation of these two basic nuclei and only the abuse of this balance can disturb this magnificent, creative harmony.

8. Aim and meaning

If the universe had remained purely material, it could just as well not exist. The mere fact of existence does not serve or explain anything. A completely dead and chaotic world would remain aimless, meaningless, and inconsequential. If galaxies, stars, and atoms had no purpose other than simple being, they might as well be absent. The universe, similarly as any other mechanism, acquires meaning only by having a purpose! But if so, what could this purpose be?

If the conclusions above are right and reality indeed has a spiritual-material character, then the rationale for the creation of consecutive universes is a natural activity of a spiritual factor which finds its ultimate justification in the person of the Absolute. It is expressed by the transformation of His ideas into real, material events and their verification in life. The method is universal evolution aimed to transform passive, dispersed energy into an initially lifeless and meaningless cosmos together with its stars and planets into a stage for the oncoming drama of life.

But this drama is not exactly planned, it is not a movie where the intrigue and the end are decided in advance and well-known before the beginning of the show. It is rather a general concept realized in the course of action and constantly adapted to changing conditions. It is not an engine where all the parts fit exactly together, but rather a Gothic cathedral erected over hundreds of years by consecutive builders. The basic concept is consequently continued, but the details are subject to accidents, modifications, and complementation. We, too, participate in it because, while being one of the aims of the universe, we are also a means to achieve them. As an aim, we have been anticipated already in the preconditions of the project; but as coworkers, we have a certain degree of independence. As one of the local incarnations of the universal idea of a being who possesses a soul, we have the possibility to shape our own surroundings – but also to make our own mistakes. However, if we make too many of them, then our earthly experiment may fail. Universal evolution maintains a planned direction, but the fate of particular planets depends also on the cooperation of intelligent persons. The Absolute supervises the continuity of the whole enterprise; but reduces His personal involvement to exceptional cases only. This does not, however, mean that we can do whatever we want.

There is still the question of why Cosmic Evolution is better that one, single act of creation? One of the reasons is that large and complex enterprises should never be designed by one person or by one team. Even the most talented architect designing a large city cannot replace the intellectual freedom of decisions taken by variety of people. The principle aim designed by one distinctive mind must be enriched (in the course of further development) by the involvement of actual users. All new cities designed by one single person turned out to be monotonous and boring.

On the other hand, towns that have been developing for centuries via the shared inventiveness of thousands of individuals having different objectives, talents, and abilities and who want to get the best possible solution in a given circumstances try to find a compromise between conflicting private and public interests and to adapt to practical possibilities.

A similar rule obligates in the Grand Project of the Universe. The long evolution with a clearly described final goal carried out through the participation of partial accident and endless number of individual decisions must bring a much richer effect than one person planning. Another reason is the necessity to secure the possession of free will for intelligent beings. The consequences of a detail planning of the universe would be strict program limiting freedom of thought. And this will include limitations of the free development of the soul and will consequently limit its possibilities of the next reincarnations.

The Absolute is the creator of the order of the universe, but He is *not* the sole reason of its existence. The universe, as every outstanding piece of art, technology, or a scientific discovery, has a value in itself; independently from the benefit and satisfaction given to its author. The Absolute did not create the universe solely for himself, or for His glory, but also for values hidden in the work itself. Of them the most important are life and the soul.

It is rather doubtful that the Absolute decided to abandon His "splendid isolation" for the sake of a lifeless universe consisting of gases and minerals; not too different from the state before the act of creation. Only a living universe becomes worthy of the interest of the Highest Mind. What advantage could come from even the most excellent work without the possibility of sharing thoughts and feelings with some other intelligent beings? Why create anything in complete loneliness, knowing that it will never be seen or needed by anyone? Even the most perfect, independent, and unconditionally free person would not feel well in such circumstances. Everyone needs periodic solitude, but certainly not everlasting loneliness in the endless emptiness of cosmic space! Of what benefit is it to have all these superior attributes while being completely lonely, living only for Himself and without any problems to solve? From a human point of view, that seems very unlikely. Only the appearance of independently thinking, free persons provides meaning to the existence of the universe!

But what could their assignment be? Once having been endowed with life, a soul, and free will they cannot remain merely obedient instruments. By definition, they must be autonomous individuals with the possibility to rise to the upper spiritual class; voluntarily and by their own effort. They have not been created to be ruled over or to be tested as submissive servants, but to have an opportunity to take a part in building a better and more spiritual universe! This gives them an opportunity to rise, even for a while, above their own mediocrity, to experience great feelings – love, the joy of creation, and suffering – and to ascend, even for an instant, to the height of the Absolute. These moments justify the billions of years of development which were needed to achieve it. The true meaning of these emotions is greater than their actual reasons because only then can human beings, for a blink of an eye, come close to the goal of their existence. At such moments, despite of all their shortcomings, they reach the peak of their possibilities.

But there must be still other reasons for the existence of the world. We cannot, on our low level, discern all of them, but we can assume that they result from the logic of the construction common for the whole cosmos. I shall list below only those which seem to be the most likely:

The first is the natural activity of the spiritual component of reality expressed by the Absolute's creative way of life. The second, the materialization of His ideas; third, the origin and development of life and the soul, fourth, the harmony and beauty of nature understood as a work of art. Fifth is the preservation of the constant, unending activity of being in a state of equilibrium between opposite forces: existence and nonexistence, construction and destruction, eternity and fleetingness, and the everlasting renewal of life and ceaselessly returning death.

The ultimate aim of the present (and of each next) universe is not a state of permanent excellence, but the gradual realization of objectives and values that can come into being during its existence. The goal is *not* the transformation of reality into a purely spiritual one, because such a world simply could not exist – similarly as an exclusively material one. Therefore the end of the present (and of every other) universe will not be the end of everything that exists. Complete nothingness is impossible and will never happen. Eternity is pointless and for that reason it cannot change into an endless, enduring, stagnant state of affairs or (even less) into progress without the end. The only possibility left is a cyclic reappearance of periods of the passive dispersion of energy and of active endeavor to achieve maximal perfection via the cyclic repetition of births and deaths, creation and destruction, development and fall, the growth of energy and exhaustion of forces, visible all over the universe in all scales of time and magnitude.

In this perspective *there is no* place for an apocalypse understood as total destruction of the present order planned by higher forces and preceding the victory of good over evil and of spirit over matter! The vision of an everlasting *Kingdom of God* cannot be reconciled with the concept of a purposefully and harmoniously developing universe having a beginning and an end. The solely existing, kinetic, and constantly developing reality never will change into eternally lasting, static excellence. All that could be achieved are transient states of the most possible harmony of these two elements. Increasing the share of spirit in everyday life does not increase the value of life, as such, but does elevate its intellectual-emotional quality. Each current incarnation is as important as the former or the next. There will never be any ultimate victory of spirit over matter, because matter, as an unavoidable component of reality, will always be present – though not as the opposition of spirit, but as its complementation.

Because the life of thinking persons is *not* evaluated on the basis of their submissiveness to the Absolute, but on their share in realizing the *idea of an independent being possessing soul*, there is no place here for the notion of shared responsibility for *original sin*, and consequently, for the redemption of the whole of humanity. Nobody was born with a "sinful nature," and the whole species of *homo sapiens* has never been submitted to one symbolic, collective test of obedience, but only to, repeating in every life, individual tests of reason and consciousness. Each particular individual must pass a personal examination from each following life; but the entire species of humankind must pass only the collective test of common sense, and show an ability to survive in consecutive inherited environments till the fulfillment of its destiny. It can therefore be assumed that the only possible collective responsibility may refer to the fate of the whole species living on a given planet.

There will be no *Final Judgment* and no division into the saved and condemned, because the only ones left will be those who, by way of consecutive reincarnations, achieved the state of highest-possible perfection. When further growth will be impossible, no more embodiments will be needed or desired. By the end of this long sojourn all souls will join the Absolute to pass to Him their personal experiences, which will be included into the design of the next universe. And this will assure them an indirect share in the everlasting life of the Absolute.

Yes, there is a certain similarity to the Christian concept, but much more to Origen's philosophy than to official canons. But these disparities are substantial – e.g., that we cannot be *"condemned"* for lack of faith in God (in this case in Yahve) without even being aware of his existence.

Presently, at the beginning of the 21st century, only about 25% of humanity is Christian, the rest consists of followers of different religions or of atheists. The image of a god who creates new human souls knowing that 75% of them will land in hell – a sort of eternal concentration camp – is obviously false and in conflict with basic justice. Much more likely is that all those who fail to observe the principles of the harmony of being may expect only painless dissolution in an all-embracing spiritual sphere. Like those who burn down the Great Amazonian Forest and refuse responsibility for the steady decline of the world's reserve of oxygen. They are guilty of negligence in cooperating with the Absolute in the work to maintain the harmony of being. Faith in God alone, even sincere, cannot replace practical results of such an activity and does not prevent its negative influence on the rest of living world. Motivation of the Absolute is **not** to confirm His existence by commitment of less mature beings, but to bring His project to an successful end. We receive then the following chain of dependences:

The soul in order to fulfill its purpose must be free and even capable of bearing responsibility for the self-destruction of the group or civilization she belongs and finally for the whole planet. Without this there is no positive selection and therefore goal-directed development on all of these levels.

The ultimate end of the present universe will come when the natural possibilities for further spiritual growth will have been completely exhausted. The unity of spirit and matter will break down and the reality composed of both will fade away. Matter will return to dispersed chaos and life and spirit to the Absolute. Time will stop to flow, reincarnation will end, and the Absolute will enter a state of maximally-possible spirituality and contemplation. He will then begin a period of lonely, purely intellectual existence dedicated to inventing new ideas and preparing for the next Great Cosmic Enterprise. Such a break may last either billions of years or only a second. Then the light will flash again; and everything will start from the beginning. A new universal evolution will start the materialization of an idea for the next universe. However, it will not be a duplicate of what was before, but a new, original, equally beautiful and interesting oeuvre. This is because the Absolute, as a talented and endlessly original artist, never repeats His concepts.

9. Recognition of good and bad

The most crucial criteria of good and bad stem from the nature of the universe. Their original source is the rational, well-disposed, and impartial mind of the Absolute and their objective is to build a better, more spiritual, beautiful, and interesting world.

We do not know exactly what His plans are, but we can guess them from the direction of the hitherto development of the universe. The measure of values is clear and closely depends on the influence on the further growth of the spiritual sphere of reality. All what is favorable to progress from simple to complex, from lifeless to alive, and from thoughtless to thinking is good and all that is harmful to it is bad. This criterion stems from the very essence of the universe as an entity existing in the form of continuous creative evolution; it is also authentic, objective, and always binding.

The most important ideas preconditioning the origin and realization of all others are the ideas of life and the soul. But life requires the presence of clearly specified physical conditions, and the soul of clearly specified spiritual conditions. Consequently, the first criterion of separation between good and evil arises from the necessity to preserve a physical and spiritual environment that is favorable to the development of life and the soul. This may be described by the following definition:

The good is all that is favorable for the existence and protection of an environment favorable to the realization of the concepts of life and the soul. All that is contrary to this is wrong.

This principle is universal, unconditionally binding and obligatory everywhere and every time. It contains the essence of natural law, is recognized by mind, heart, intuition and confirmed by reason and practical application. It arises from the following logical sequence of causes and effects:

There is no morality without conscience, no conscience without the soul, no soul without a body, no body without life, no life without a harmony of the physical and spiritual environment.

To summarize – there are no moral values without harmony of the physical and spiritual environment. In this sequence each successive condition requires completion of the former. The maintenance of the harmony of the physical environment favorable to life is a necessary condition for the emergence and development of life, the soul, and conscience – and ultimately of the further progress of the universe. I want to stress that this chain of dependences relates to factually and currently existing reality, and therefore is mandatory without regard to one's personal stance or the political attitude of the observer. This testifies that moral values in their deepest essence are non-relative and result from the basic structure of the world.

Just as life requires a certain physical environment, the soul needs a specific human environment – one providing freedom of thought and action, mutual benevolence, honesty, and an active intellectual atmosphere. Taken together, these features may be called "spiritual harmony". Ultimately, then, the development of the soul depends on external conditions. The state of harmony of natural and human environments becomes an inevitable, non-relative condition of its further spiritual growth. In the nature this harmony is maintained by a self-adjusting ecological mechanism; but in the world modified by humans it relies on human activity. We have here a mutual dependence and subtle balance: further growth of the soul depends on the good will and intelligence of those who have already achieved a sufficient level of self-awareness. This makes the way up difficult, strenuous, and demanding, but the smallest slip can be enough to send it down to the starting point. But despite this we still improve! Once we are free from the burden of common guilt for some mythical former sins, we will begin to be individually responsible for our personal fate only. And this opens the way to endless advancement in the course of upward, universal, spiritual evolution.

Physical and spiritual harmony taken together make *the harmony of the world*. That is, the state of reality in conformity with the intentions of the Absolute, necessary for the existence of all living creatures; and particularly indispensable for their higher forms. This harmony consists of such obvious factors as a clean natural environment, physical health, freedom, a feeling of safety, moderate material well-being, mutual benevolence and empathy – together with the corresponding mental level. All these factors influence and complement each other. Ultimately, most the most universal criteria for the distinction of good and evil can be brought down to the following:

Everything that contributes to the harmony of the world is good, and everything averse to it is evil.

This is the absolute, objective, the ultimate common denominator and starting point for the formulation of all other criteria for the distinction between good and evil, which bind all intelligent beings living in the universe. It marks the general character of all other rules; every other criterion must be judged against this principle.

The traditional phrase that the world has been created for the *greater glory of God* should be understood as a metaphor stressing the talent of the creator and the visible beauty and coherence of the whole opus. Each, albeit temporary, disturbance of this state may result in the disruption of biological and spiritual evolution, and in the subsequent regression from the order already achieved. In the case of an individual person it could bring illness or death, and in the case of a whole society – war, revolution, or ecological disaster.

Life stands for the undeniable, superior value and condition of existence of all other values. The necessity to protect it imposes certain objective and non-relative moral principles. These principles do not arise from a revealed truth or personal recommendations given by some supernatural power, but from the very structure of the world. Please notice that the Ten Commandments from the Bible, (like: "do no kill ") are almost identical in all religions all over the world. This wide-spread similarity testifies to the presence of intuitively felt universal moral values lying at the foundations of the whole cosmic enterprise. They are verifiable practically because they refer not only to life in general, but to every single life. They obviously need an intelligent interpretation of exceptions and necessities. It is always bad to wage war or torture people but sometimes is impossible to avoid casualties while fighting in defense of one's own life and freedom. They are many other circumstances requiring one to choose the lesser evil, e.g., when the preservation of one life demands the sacrifice of another. But even in these cases, losses and suffering must be limited to the necessary minimum.

The orderly world conveys to us certain, immanent principles of behavior. Since our own existence is derivative of the universal order, the recognition and implementation of these rules is an obvious condition for the survival of individuals and society. The human being as a creation of nature cannot use himself as a point of reference or become fully independent from all that has created him. From this comes the next rule:

Moral criteria set up by humans are always subjective and modified to fit the interest of groups and individuals. The only impartial moral judgments are those which refer to natural laws originating from the structure of the world.

We cannot assign to ourselves the role of the sole source of values while assuming that the surrounding environment is accidental, indifferent, and totally deprived of any values. Such a basic logical mistake must bring catastrophe in all realms – environmental, cultural, social, and personal. As a species, we do not possess enough wisdom and goodness to overcome the disproportions between our primitive instincts and the practical talents which made possible the invention of the atomic bomb, the poisoning of oceans, deforestation, and runaway population growth. There is no freedom without responsibility. Not only towards other people, but before the laws of nature that were set up by the Highest Mind – whoever He is. They are obligatory for all of us, including also those who negate His existence.

What then are the practical conclusions? Indeed, nothing new. Everything has been already said by philosophers and theologians and repeated a million times by many others. It can be summarized in one sentence: *behave decently, honestly and with good will in relation to other people and to nature!*

10. Perspectives

This chapter contains a search for a road that allows joining the principal ideas of Christianity with a theistic image of the world that is independent from any other religion. I realize that some of the conclusions drawn here disagree with the official stance of Great Christian Churches, but I think that friendly, rationally-justified theism is better than complete indifference. Since I am not able to believe in everything that the Church recommends, and I do not want to become one more accidental object in an accidentally-emerged world, I have to construct my own standpoint, risking the commission of all possible mistakes.

I shall start with the question: how can we recognize which of the many religions is closest to the truth? The most reliable, objective criterion could be the quality of civilization which has been developed in relation with a given religion. And so far, this examination was passed best by Christianity, which has contributed to the creation of the most dynamic civilization in the history of humankind.

All other civilizations have borrowed so much from this one that they became its local variations. Its attractiveness has also been proved by millions of people who, from different parts of the world, try to relocate to Europe or to other countries of the Christian-European tradition. One can confidently say that, in spite of all the mistakes committed, the results of 2000 years of existence of Christianity are decisively positive. All attempts to replace it by atheistic political ideas or by religious sects have proved catastrophic. The positive effects of Christian values are clearly visible and can be objectively proved without any use of supernatural arguments. The practical achievements confirmed by the experiment lasting 1,500 years (therefore in its essence scientific) are more convincing that all the accompanying mistakes. Let us remember that there are no absolutely perfect human works.

It is, however, high time to admit openly that only a fraction of Jesus' followers actually believe all that was written in the Bible. This creates a situation that requires some widely-designed changes of traditionally understood notions; remembering, however, that the foundation of further survival and development of Christianity must remain its most evident leading idea – that is, the imperative of justice, love, benevolence, and peace. These values are plain, practically confirmed, and accepted by all reasonably thinking people, whenever and wherever they live. Their validity is permanent and independent from both a literary and symbolic understanding of the Holy Scriptures.

The meaning of the Gospel is not diminished if some of its fragments are perceived as poetic metaphors or literary ornamentations written to stimulate readers' imagination. Although the circumstances and customs in most of these narrations belong to another epoch, many of them still contain undeniable values and serve as an example of behavior.

This is not to suggest a change in the Gospel, but to see in it also as poetry addressed to our hearts. However (independently of this), regaining the confidence of more skeptical individuals requires clarification and official separation of the things that may be considered true from those which are mere metaphors. Consequently, the association of the Bible with Christianity shall be limited to the four Gospels only, as they are the basic source of knowledge about the intentions and teaching of Jesus Christ. Accordingly, the Old Testament should be considered a historically essential and important step forward on the road to monotheism, but nevertheless external and belonging to another religion. This would be a simple consequence of the quite different atmosphere and character of these two texts. Many followers would accept this change with relief and as an affirmation of the conclusion they have already independently reached. This would definitely contribute to clarification of the present situation, because no religion based on conventional truth can any longer be convincing.

After two-thousand years, Christianity shall become a separate and fully-independent religion, based on its own message, and on a different attitude to reality. It will thus make its meaning clearer and its relations with Judaism better. We would no longer be like a pair of former spouses who, after divorce, continue to live in the same house – the opportunity for any difference in opinion will pass away, and the window for true friendship will open wider. I want once more to underline that this is not a critique, but simple acknowledgement of fundamental division between these two concepts. Judaism will still remain what it is now – one of the great religions of the world, like Buddhism or Islam, representing the road to comprehension of reality characteristic for a certain time of history. All problems associated with adapting Christianity to the present situation remain its own internal affair, independent from any other creed.

This would not bring as great an earthquake as might be expected. The Anglican Church, so strongly linked with the Old Testament, has lost (within one generation only) about 90% of its followers. At the same time, the losses within Catholicism (where the O.T. is held at much greater distance) have been incomparably smaller.

If Christianity wants to survive, it must separate these two narratives and offer a more comprehensive image of the world. The faith of today's person cannot be too far removed from the opinions he is ready to accept. He cannot believe in tolerance and democracy in his secular life, and in absolute monarchy in his religious one. To be an independent and autonomous personality and at the same time a fearful and obedient subject. To recognize human rights but to acquiesce with mass repressions and punishments for a minor disobedience. To believe that humans have received absolute authority over nature and to realize that they are only its part, subject to the same limitations. It is no longer possible to assent to an image of the Absolute as the impartial father of all people with the picture of a warrior who promised his chosen subjects dominion over all others. It is illogical to ask him for help in conquering someone else's territory and at the same time to believe in his love for the whole of humanity.

There are still some people who need literary metaphor as an ornamentation of truth, but there are also others, who cannot take it. And they should not be forced to choose whether to reject Christianity altogether or to be obligated to believe in episodes contradictory to what they consider common sense. The best way out would be to regard this question as of secondary importance and to agree that particular individuals may choose their own version, without being criticized or excluded from the community or separated from an excellent cultural tradition. After all, there is no evidence that miracles happen, but nor is there evidence that miracles are always contradictory with nature. Perhaps there are some still undiscovered physical laws that permit some of them. Three hundred years ago television would have been considered supernatural.

The brutal truth is that Christianity cannot afford a further outflow of believers. If in Western Europe the proportion of people who consider themselves Christians has shrunk from 60% to about 10%, how much time left before they will become a small, insignificant sect? Therefore, the first objective is to get these people back by offering them contemporary arguments for the existence of God comprehended as a really existing Highest Mind responsible for the order of the universe. As the force whose presence is verifiable by experience of everyday life! Let us remember that there are very few true or genuine atheists! Most of them will accept modern metaphysical arguments with relief, on condition that they will not be obligated to believe in things they are not able to believe. Such reasoning must of course be served without use of pompous language, so annoying today. What they really need is a rationally justified return to a logically built world and to non-relative morality. As well as to grasp that materialism *is* ***not*** *the only truthful and scientific viewpoint*, because science confirms that the ever so close correlation of all components of reality cannot be accidental. And everyday life provides testimony that immaterial thoughts and feelings – that is, the soul – determine our behavior.

I am not talking about bringing the canons of faith to the level of skeptics, but about the necessity to prevent the exodus of those who do not follow all expectations. About the necessity to accept as Christians all skeptics of good will who identify Christianity with the culture they have grown up in, rather than with uncritical faith. Fairness of widely-recognized benevolence and decency would not change if we considered Jesus Christ to be only a man who, thanks to His outstanding moral sensitivity, was able to comprehend this and to pass it on to others.

After all, He never called himself God, but rather "Son of the father who is in heaven"; and several times mentioned that He "was sent" by him, but never about any kind of personal meeting. It seems obvious that He did not try to transfer human family relations to the upper, divine level, but rather to find a way to the minds of listeners by using understandable similarities.

The fact that His disciples considered Him to be God (Thomas, Peter & John in the gospels; and others in the epistles) represents a purely personal, subjective version of events. His declaration about His identity with the father" (*"I and the Father are one"* – John 10:30), has either symbolic meaning or is a later addition adapted during theological debates in the early ages of Christianity.

This resulted in the official proclamation of two most difficult and controversial dogmas: first, that God, despite being a spirit, can have a human-like family, and second that the son and the father are the same person. What is more, they are equal and identical with the third person – a mysterious entity called the Holy Spirit. The impossibility to understand this enigmatic scheme forces sceptics either to give up common sense or to leave Christianity and choose a painfully simplistic, but much more logical materialism. If the Church's founders had proposed a simpler definition, like: *"Jesus was only a man who was inspired by God"* this problem would not exist, but His principal message would be still the same as now: *"Stop hating and killing each other, do not be so greedy, egoistic, and aggressive, try to be good and loving. Remember that you are guardians of the rest of the living world, not its ruthless exploiter. Pursue peace and moderation! Change the present course of your civilization before it will be too late!".*

Surprisingly, today, 2000 years later, these principles are as pressing as then! But in present circumstances Jesus' mission has been changed from severe judge of humanity as a whole into a compassioned guardian protecting us from ourselves! If we do not want to perish, we must ascend independently and significantly higher than we have been able to do so far.

Once more I wish to stress that this is not an attempt to intrude into the present dogma of the faith.. This book is written for skeptics like me, who are not sincere atheists, but who, despite many objections, want to remain within the perimeters of Christianity. But how to do so? The model of the world proposed here is an attempt to find the most probable answer to this question.

There is of course a doubt as to what degree this picture remains in accord, at least in the general sense, with such fundamental Christian beliefs as Salvation, the Incarnation, and the Resurrection. The first difficulty appears when we try to consent to the proposed here image of the Absolute as: *the most perfect of all possible incarnations of the idea of life and soul* with any kind of a concrete and true human personality. It is rather doubtful that our abstractive Highest Mind would like to become a human being, and to demean itself to the rank of beings that are still on the lowest level of spiritual development. And even less to become a member of an untypical human family as a son of a human mother and of the "Father who is in heaven", with whom He is, in some way, *coexistent*. In the official complicated definition of the Holy Trinity, the only notion of the Holy Spirit seems to be sufficiently abstract to be considered as equivalent to the Highest Mind. All this shows that the image of the Absolute given above is still far from traditional image of the Christian God.

From this point of view *"Salvation"* may be understood as a natural and necessary change of the course of civilization, providing it with a new meaning and significance. That is rescuing humanity not only from *"penalty for the past sin"* but also from contradiction between our ruthless, human egoism and distinctive practical talent which lets us change the environment. Jesus' goal was to overcome human nature by the new, more civilized spirit. In the present phase of development this leads toward a fairer, gentler, and safer world. That is exactly what, thanks to the Christianization of Europe, has been partially achieved and clearly confirmed by historical facts. This makes possible the agreeable coexistence of Christianity with the model of reality presented above.

In spite of this the most important features still remain common. In both cases the universe is the materialization of an idea conceived by God (the Absolute), with the difference that, in one case, it has been created by a single act of will; and in the other, in the course of intentionally-designed evolution. Similarly, the person of Jesus Christ and His teaching remain a necessary fragment of the spiritual development of humanity; an event that had to happen at a certain moment of history. Here and there the common attribute of God and human beings is the possession of a soul; admittedly of a different quality, but of the same kind. And this is sufficient to perceive His presence and to understand His intentions. The basic history of creation is, in its essence, almost the same. *"The Word"* from the prologue to St. John's Gospel – which "In the beginning was with God and was God" (J 1.1.4, King James Bible) – is in its deepest meaning identical with the Absolute, defined in chapter 5 as "*the sole creator of original ideas and indispensable condition for the existence of life and of all remaining spiritual attributes. And in consequence, as the author of the Grand Concept of the Universe."* In both cases "the Word" (*without him was not anything made that was made"*) as well as the Absolute are *"the sole, necessary, and natural component of all including spiritual-material reality"* and condition for the existence of *"everything that is sensible and rational"* – and above all, life. Both texts express the same contents and confirm the conscious role of the spirit in the creation of the world. Similarly, neither of them imputes this spirit with any distinct form, human or other. This fundamental compliance makes all other differences less important.

There still remains the question of the Resurrection as the ultimate confirmation of the truth proclaimed by Jesus Christ. It provides the fundamental component of the Gospel, the ultimate proof of victory of life over death, and of love and benevolence over evil, intrigue, and cruelty.

But can we believe this while denying the existence of another, supernatural reality? Yes, we can because exactly in this only one, all-encompassing reality, Resurrection becomes possible! For since there is no other, "lower" or "upper" reality, all that is going on must happen in agreement with compelling laws. And above all with the law which says that initiative always belongs to the spirit and matter is merely a passive and obedient performer. And if the Resurrection were intended as a necessary "signal" given by the Absolute to humanity it would justify the use of exceptional physical laws. And despite that, in all other circumstances mortality is the necessary complementation of life, the particular importance of this event may justify this one, single exception from routine.

We must also remember that convincingly written descriptions of certain events, true or not, belong to spiritual phenomena that may bring real, material results. Even if the evangelic depiction of the Resurrection is not an accurate report of what had really happened, it still remains an idea that has positively influenced the course of history and changed material reality. If encounters with the Resurrected Christ happened only in the imagination of disciples, in the final account, they were transformed into an idea that has activated the real energy needed to perform concrete work. In this case, bringing into being a new religion which has changed the direction of European, and finally, of worldwide, civilization. Which is to say that immaterial thought started a concrete, historical process which can be studied and evaluated.

From this perspective the Resurrection became a fact – an event confirmed by its results. Its practical effects – the creation of a new powerful culture – are too great and obvious to be dismissed as a mere dream. The faith in it has changed the lives of so many people for such a long time that it serves as clear evidence that spiritual forces form physical reality and cause material changes. Even if it is a legend it will forever remain the most fruitful and promising legend !

Consequently, the question of whether the Resurrection was possible within the frame of natural laws becomes of second importance. If we consider life to be a spiritual phenomenon, then death is not only an outcome of the disintegration of the body, but also termination of cooperation between its particular soul and its particular matter. But perhaps in certain exceptional circumstances the forces of nature can reverse (at least temporarily) this process. Present attempts to prolong human life and reverse the effects of senility lean in the same direction, but never are called miracles.

Ultimately then, we may assume that the model of reality proposed here remains in basic agreement with such fundamental components of Christianity as the existence of God (the Absolute), of the universe reflecting divine order, and the possession of a potentially immortal soul. As well as the duty to observe natural law and bear the resulting personal responsibility. Therefore, there are no reasons that would not allow for the coexistence of these two points of view. They have enough in common to begin cooperation and to rescue the set of our common beliefs and even to enhance them by some new and original ideas. This perspective is certainly much more reasonable and promising than treating all "cautious Christians" with distrust and indifference or rejecting them as heretics and threatening them with hell, which they do not believe in anyway. I want to remind once more that this is not a proposal for a new faith, but rather of an intellectual attitude that could persuade those who consider Christianity an intrinsic component of European culture to remain within its realm.

One may ask here whether the claim about the particular significance of Christianity is really justified. Does it bring something special that is absent in other religions? The answer is "decisively yes, it does!" There are several arguments that speak for it! The first one is the long record of philosophical disputes inside the Church. After two-thousand years of philosophical disagreements we have achieved a state of maturity and tolerance which makes it possible to get rid of certain historically-justified, but presently inconsequential problems and concentrate on the real needs of modern humanity. Great passions are already behind us, we have ceased to cut each other's throats and become more willing to start a sober discussion. The decisive reason is that, in the course of these fights and negotiations, a complete, compact system of values has been built that is compatible with democracy and in agreement with intrinsic traits of the human species. Not everything in it is completely new, but taken as a whole, it creates a logical and consistent entirety that has serious prospects of becoming the foundation of a universal moral code. Its practical value has been sufficiently confirmed by two-thousand years of experience. What we need now is a persuasive picture of the world showing the most likely order of things as complementation of the science-inspired, materialistic perspective.

Christian civilization is exceptional because it considers all people as free, individual persons able to reach a compromise between the need of authority and the natural inclination toward individual liberty. No other civilization in the history of humankind has gone through such an intellectual experience. The principles that originated in the course of this process became a common possession of the whole of humanity, providing an indispensable, practically-verified foundation of modern civilization. I shall try now to describe those that seem the most important.

They are as follows: • the equality of all people before God and therefore before the law; • the division between civil and religious powers; • the command to love your neighbor as yourself, • the requirement of basic decency in relation with other people and with nature; •the priority to protect life as a particular gift of God, expressed by the command "you must not kill"; • the free will and dignity of human person. Following are some short comments on each of them:

1. The equality of all people before God and therefore before the law.

This statement seems obvious today, but at the time of the early Roman Empire it was revolutionary. It is true that this idea was known already in Athens and in republican Rome, but it applied only to free citizens. For the rest of them it was a time of drastic inequalities and open cruelty. Let us imagine how shocking it was for masses of poor people and slaves who for the first time in their life learned that on a basic level of humanity, they are not only equal to their masters, but even more privileged (*"But he who is greatest among you shall be your servant."* (Mat. 23:11). and because *the "Kingdom of Heaven is theirs"* (Mt.6:10). Moreover, they have the right to forgive, and by forgiving, they become closer to God and better than their oppressors.

But also today, when the principle of equal rights has become commonly (but often only seemingly) approved by most countries, the new, unexpected threats came into sight. Particularly worrying are attempts to control great human masses, and experiments on modification of the brain. Both may endanger the further existence of humanity as a collection of free individualities. Historical experience shows that only faith in the upper, divine order of the world can hold us back from using these inventions to satisfy our primitive instincts – i.e., those that were necessary in the animal phase, but became an obstacle to development in human phase. Once we begin to regard ourselves as the highest moral authority there is a justified apprehension that privileged groups will not resist temptation to improve their own (and their descendants) mental abilities. And this must bring division of humanity into genetically wise elite and stupid masses, masters and slaves.

Artificial intervention into the process of independent development is tantamount to resignation from the self-perfection of our individual soul. While replacing personal experience by artificial, external stimulations we may lose the status of coworkers of the Absolute and in the final outcome the prospect of reincarnation. This would be equal to failing a collective examination, and perhaps to complete resignation of our species from its share in the further spiritual advance of the universe. The Absolute' concept to realize the idea of a person possessing a soul on the planet Earth would end in complete failure.

We shall also remember that social movements leading toward the present conviction about the equality of all people and finally to democracy have their foundations in both Greece and Gospel. There is no doubt that the idea of elected government comes from Athens, but the notion of social justice and of equality of poor and rich before the law came from Jesus' teaching. This double heritage is unique for European culture similarly as considering personal freedom as the natural state of human life. Leftist, atheistic movements borrowed these two notions from the Christian principle of compassion for the poor and oppressed. Present scientific opinion that all things existing are made exclusively from the matter does not have any logical correlation with human rights or with any other spiritual values.

2. The division of civil and religious powers

At the time of Jesus the division of civil and religious powers was so new and revolutionary that it needed nearly two-thousand years of social progress to find general support and comprehension. In imperial Rome the notions of a god and of the sovereign were closely connected – the ruler was a god, and a god was the ruler. Negation of this was considered state treason. Particularly in occupied Israel it required great courage and independent thinking to proclaim a separation between the power of the state and divinity; and to say: *give to Caesar what is his and give to God everything that belongs to God* (Mt.22:21.)

One cannot deny that for a long time Christian Churches also claimed the right to political decision-making and authority over secular power. But in the course of history, it turned out that both sides can act quite independently without any harm for each of them. Today, at the beginning of 21st century this division has become obvious in all Christian countries; however in other parts of the world we still see the attempt to identify ideology or religion with state power. It turns out that the idea of democracy does not contain values so non-relative that they might prevent further continuation of this trend. On the contrary – it allows for a flexible interpretation of the notions of liberty and equality. Without the shared belief that a just human society is a part and reflection of some higher, universal order we will be exposed to all kinds of fanaticism and totalitarianism and together with it to slavery and spiritual fall.

3. Obligation to love your enemy and to show decent attitude in relation to other people and to nature

Equally new are two other components of Christian philosophy. The first is "Love your neighbor" (Mt 5:43) and the second is "turn the other cheek" (Mt. 6:38). Both appeared at a time when mass murders, capture of slaves, and the custom of bloody revenge lasting for generations were commonly-respected standards. Let us remember that this happened in a country where God, as well as the emperor, were expected to care for, and show mercy, only to obedient subjects while inflicting ruthless punishment on enemies; or even bring about their total annihilation. Both situations refer either to the personal interest of the suppliant, or to the nation he belongs to. The general principles of relationships with earthly powers, as well as with God, were the same: submission, flattery, and a request for attention. Politics was an exact reflection of contemporary religions – and the other way around

Christianity alone, enriched by Greek thought, has introduced the notion of a God impartial to tribal affairs and more interested in individuals than in nations. Together with an idea of a human person possessing the right to freedom and dignity resulting from the bare fact of its existence. He is no longer a humble servant, but a free, independent, and responsible individual. He does not try to get the attention of God by subservient begging for help in personal problems; but by something quite the opposite: by resignation from personal gain, and by decent behavior in relations with others by trying to understand the enemy, and to forgive vengeance.

Such an attitude is particularly needed now when democracy no longer guarantees reasonable thinking and impartiality, and any local conflict may turn into total disaster. Mass indoctrination, control of information, and manipulation of minds deprive people of the ability to critically think, and therefore, from making the right choices. The conclusion is clear – the Christian idea of forgiveness is no longer a personal option, but a political program and necessary condition of survival.

4. Priority to protect life as a particular gift of God, as expressed by the command: "you must not kill", and by the rule: "Live and let live"

No other religion says it so explicitly as Christianity. The introduction of this rules into global awareness is an obvious condition of the further development of an intelligently designed world. It is always valid, practically verifiable, and in agreement with reason and intuition. Particularly today, when the further growth of the global population is starting to overcome the capacity of the natural environment; and when the capability of killing each other so often overcomes the ability to find a reasonable compromise. That is why the renewal of Christianity, in its pacifistic and more intellectually-convincing form, has become a historical necessity. In an age of atomic and biological weapons, the explicit condemnation of ***every*** aggression and of every war is no longer a question of local interest, but a condition for the further survival of the human species. One cannot expect that awareness of this will change human nature, and wars will completely disappear. But when it becomes a permanent and principal objective of Christianity, those who reject such a command will be clearly responsible for the subsequent disasters. And this shall bring a change in the way of thinking. Not mentioning that the experience of using modern weapons and the subsequent sufferings of millions should be more convincing than propaganda used to justify bloody and senseless ideological or religious conflicts. At least for those who are able to think!

5. Free will and dignity of the human person as indispensable conditions for democracy

It is self-evident that a truly democratic society must consist of people who are free; and possess a sense of responsibility not only for themselves, but also for their community. This is possible only thanks to self-awareness about the possession of soul and as consequence of free will. It is however worth to remember that every determination (e.g., by physical force, fear, propaganda, or other kind of manipulation) limits or excludes freedom – and consequently, responsibility. This also refers to faith in complete submission to (these or other) upper forces who have total control over reality, and of our conduct. Therefore, every religion favorable to democracy must openly admit that human beings are capable by their own effort and act of will to cooperate with God in the creation of the world.

This applies to personal freedom as well as to the common good. Such an understanding of their own share in shaping reality provides the human person with the natural dignity; that *of being worthy of honor or respect* that *cannot be taken away from him.* Discussion about the range of human freedom has gone on within Christianity for two thousand years, but if it wants to be the religion of the future it must confirm this condition clearly and without insinuations. Meticulous, permanent care and intervention from above is neither needed nor desired by those who have the ambition to conquer the cosmos.

All these conditions are met by a Christian culture which successfully conjoins the European pursuit of freedom, with ancient Greek thought and the message of the Gospel. It was, therefore, not an accident that democratic states and free societies developed within the range of its influence. The experience of the last 100 years indicates that all attempts to replace it by official materialism has led to depriving individuals of freedom and dignity for the sake of a "beloved leader", "power of the people", or some other ideology. The removal of Christianity always results in the reduction of free society to closely-controlled masses; and is typically accompanied by physical and intellectual terror, fear, poverty, and eventually, war. The experiences prove that together with losing the possibility to execute our freedom of thinking and therefore an opportunity to develop our souls, civilization slides down in the hierarchy of being to the level of non-living items.

Looking back, Jesus appears to be a farsighted lawmaker, philosopher, and insightful judge of human nature; whose moral standards outshone those of His time. By combining already-known norms with He demanded respect for everyone, and repudiation of hostility (Mt.5.26), He provides the conditions humanity must observe in order to rise above its hitherto development. No matter, then, whether His presence on Earth was a result of divine intervention in history: the practical results of His activity are certainly real and verifiable. They still remain the crucial and necessary condition for the continuation and development of our civilization.

The principal condition for the renewal of Christianity is resignation from the image of God who uses wars as a tool of reward and punishment; giving victories to "his own" people, and calamity to the others. The tradition of seeing God as a warrior, as someone who takes part in human conflicts or gives military advice, is not only unjust and extremely naïve, ~~as~~ it also (and more importantly) contributes to the incoherence of the whole picture. Texts presenting the conquest of someone else's territory with the help of "our" God can no longer remain a part of Christian doctrine because they destroy it from the inside. One does not have to be particularly smart to notice that the impartial Absolute, who feels empathy toward the whole universe, cannot (at the same time) be the chief of a tribe of wandering shepherds. And ~~that~~ the motto "God is love" is clearly opposite to the image of someone who helps conquer cities, murders their entire population, or punishes the whole of humanity by deluge, just because it has not risen to his expectations.

The denunciation of this tradition became necessary to maintain the coherency of the philosophical concept of Christianity. Further tolerance of double standards will promote the departure of all critically thinking people. Anyway, it is contrary to the Gospel. It has been clearly said that: *But let your words be: Yes, yes; no, no; for whatsoever is more than these comes of evil* (Mt.5.37). Tolerance of such double-thinking has become one of the reasons for leaving the Church. In order to stop this exodus, the Church must officially pronounce what has to be believed in, and what can be considered poetic metaphor. There is no doubt that today traditional stress on a literal understanding of biblical narrations conflicts with the expectations of the authors.

Solving our everyday problems requires the harmonious cooperation of the four realms we live in: individual and social, spiritual and material. The last hundred years have proved that materialism is not able to provide such harmony. This task requires the cooperation of a clear, rational mind, and a compassionate heart. Cold calculation alone will not tell us what to do about the widening gap between technological progress and the downward spiral of culture and morality.

11. Conclusions

All religions are right, but at the same time wrong. They are right in their deepest essence – that is, in acknowledgement of the share of a higher creative force in the order of the universe. But they are also wrong to the degree in which they are convinced about their unconditional rightness. Particularly when they offer a precise image of their own God and provide detailed prescriptions on how to live in accordance with rules supposedly revealed personally by Him. And when they maintain that such knowledge has been revealed to certain chosen persons during their personal meetings with Him or with His messengers. But they are their worst when trying to convert others by imposing their own dogma by force – in its essence this equals replacing one myth by another that is equally impossible to verify.

Forced conversion arouses hatred; which, in turn, leads to unrelenting, intolerant wars, destruction of advanced civilizations, and disasters. Since religion provides a shape to the whole of culture, these wars never end – like the old conflict between Islam and Christianity that has already lasted over a thousand years. Its present phase is no good for us. One-hundred years of aggressive materialism brought the biological decline that has left the old, atheistic Europe obsessed by leftist liberalism without the spiritual force necessary to oppose the deep faith of young Muslim countries. This gives them hope for an easy victory. Today, in the middle of 2019 we face a new chapter of this tragedy.

If we want to survive this oncoming danger we must find endorsement in something that is reasonable, but greater than ourselves. And this requires setting up a solid theistic foundation based on intellect rather than on emotion; and more on observation than on revelation. One that would let us change our present faith into justified conviction about the existence of the Absolute resulting from examination and interpretation of the sensibly-organized world surrounding us. This means resignation from complete certitude for the benefit of greater probability and agreement that our knowledge will forever remain limited.

At first glance this looks difficult; but does not the majority of those who consider themselves Christians feel the same? Such a standpoint would not provide us with the absolute truth; but will let us see the most likely outline of reality, and to remain moderately optimistic. This can be even easier because it does not exclude our hopes for the preservation of our soul and its future participation in the creation of the universe. The natural outcome of this attitude is the tolerance of other perceptions; with an obvious exception for those who pretend to be the only ones who are right; or try to impose their beliefs by coercion or intended manipulation of facts. And in effect, the rejection of all the inequitable gods who provide exceptional rights for their own followers only.

The question arises as to whether this kind of a restrained, "emotionally lukewarm" faith is possible at all? Of course it is, and it already exists! On this kind of foundation have been built great civilizations of the Far East. I think here about Confucian religious philosophy based on conviction that our constantly changing world is joined by oppositions that create a harmonic, organic and perfect whole. This belief does not come from revelation or faith in events from the faraway past, but from observation of reality and common sense. This point of view allowed China for thousands of years to successfully develop and to survive the tragic period of the Cultural Revolution. The present recovery stems, to significant degree, from the same tradition. We have then a practical example of long-lasting material and spiritual growth without religious wars, revelations, and other miraculous happenings, based on similar kind of attitude as has been proposed here.

This does not, however, mean that we have to remain within the same borders. A long time ago we have drawn conclusion that since the harmony of the world exists, it must have its own cause! And this brings us back to the mysterious Absolute, and obligates us to try to explain (still maintaining realism and sobriety) the purpose of the world and our role in it. To create a compact logical system linking together the idea of the immortal soul with free will, and an Evangelical compassion for others. This system obliges us to be an active component of the universal, spiritual-material reality, and to observe morality that reflects the structure of the universe.

I realize that this is not a proposition that could attract the crowd; but it may still appeal to a small percentage of people who are interested in this subject and have inclinations for critical thinking. Unfortunately, they are, as practice shows, a small minority even in the present age of dynamic exchange of information

12. The future

The paradox of our times is that the political unification of Europe is proceeding ahead together with the exhaustion of the spiritual reserves of the civilization created here. This applies not only to the continent itself, but to all societies of European origin. It is a result of the systematic laicization of European culture, which, along with surrendering the shared

Christian bond, is losing its previous dynamism. Christianity, in its present form, has ceased to be the driving force of progress; and so far, nothing has emerged that could replace it. All the attempts to fill the vacuum with political religions have proven disastrous. We do not have any shared, positive idea we would be willing to fight for – and even less to die for. The lack of confidence in our own values makes us less numerous, older, tired, and, in effect, helpless in the face of the very real dangers approaching. We do not have anything that can move our hearts and give us strength to build a new, magnificent world and still preserve our identity.

Therefore, the basic condition for Europe's renaissance is to shift the spiritual sphere to the center of cultural interest. But what does this really mean? The first thing to be done is to prove that materialism *is not* the sole *scientific* opinion worthy of modern man, because, when applied in practice, it has turned out to be unable to solve most of humanity's problems. And a theory that cannot be verified experimentally is not scientific. The second is to propose such an explanation of reality that, while being in agreement with science, will liberate us from the historical burden of religious myths. Practically, this means a return to the old outlook that the fate of planet Earth (and of all humanity) is part of an order of the universe, planned by some higher forces; and is therefore subject to the laws of this order. This opinion has been already supported by a scientifically-confirmed argument about the purposeful direction of universal evolution (the first positive approximation between physics and metaphysics). This is also the time to remind Europeans that they still have a soul what makes them responsible for their deeds. The epoch of rights without obligations, and of careless hedonism, is coming to an end; and we must return to treating life as a serious matter.

In order to explain what I mean, I shall return for a moment to history. The civilization which (in spite of internal wars) permitted Europe to lead the world was a product of compromise between Christianity and the rational, secular viewpoint. Notwithstanding its clear message of peace and benevolence, military conquests were considered a legitimate and natural political method for expanding territories and resolving conflicts. What is more, the annexation of other countries, and even whole continents, was justified by missions of conversion and the introduction of progress. We shall also remember that the greatest and most bloody wars took place in Europe among already-Christian nations.

All this was feasible as long as faith was strong, weapons primitive, and the resulting destructions relatively moderate. Christian hierarchy overlooked, however, the moment when modern weapons became so dangerous that the suffering and massive killing of civilians and soldiers could no longer justify war as a way to resolve conflicts. The contradiction between the Christian message of shared, mutual love and such destructive warfare became so drastic that it could no longer be tolerated.

The moment of trial came with the visible indifference shown by all Christian denominations in the face of the approaching First World War. The senseless death of millions of young men fallen on the battlefields like Verdun became a more effective argument against religion than all the Bolshevik propaganda. If, in 1914 (that is, in still-Christian Europe), an all-European union of Great Christian Churches had emerged that decisively opposed war, it could probably have prevented that senseless catastrophe. Nothing like this happened – most of the clergy supported idea of war *in defense of faith and fatherland.* The direct effect of this negligence was the first, massive outflow of the faithful and sudden growth of new secular religions that turned out to be even more fanatical, combative, and dangerous.

The second, even larger, mistake was the lack of ultimate, logical conclusions that should be drawn from the invention of the atomic bomb. Despite the full and general awareness that it could bring, at any moment, *mutually-assured destruction,* the nuclear countries did not resign from the notion of "just war". All great denominations still demand faith in the belligerent biblical God who uses war as a tool of reward and punishment; and takes one side of the conflict.

To this day there is no visible effort to adjust the interpretation of the Old Testament to these new, so completely changed conditions. There is precious little awareness that the situation has changed drastically; and now the further survival of nations does not depend on winning war, but on avoiding it. The best proof that the mechanism of self-preservation of "homo sapiens" has not matured to the current situation is the fact that some countries possessing atomic weapons have officially declared they would use them in the case of foreign invasion. There was no example, however, of mass opposition by the population of such a country despite that in the case of a real conflict it will be the most exposed to nuclear retaliation. This means that we are ready to kill tens of millions of people (including ourselves) for purely political reasons, or under the pressure of propaganda. In this situation, every local war may change into the last war of "all against all".

Considering the fact that, by the end of the 20th century, the number of rockets able to carry nuclear, chemical, and biological warheads was large enough to bring death to the whole of humanity ("overkill"), it became quite obvious that regarding war as an *"alternative way to carry on politics"* must, sooner or later, bring worldwide catastrophe. Its probability grows along with the range of rockets, number of local wars, and paranoid politicians. How long may this state last – one that by its very nature is temporary?

In this situation even the greatest sympathy does not justify the indifference and passivity of the Great Christian Churches in the face of the coming danger. This is tantamount to leaving the further existence of the world to a happy coincidence. Christianity does not have the right to such a lack of concern when the alternative is the end of civilization. Remembering the possibility of total annihilation and its own message of love and peace, Christianity should decisively struggle to achieve complete abolition of war ***(every war)*** as a legal tool to achieve political aims. As well as for the introduction of a worldwide treaty that will proclaim military aggression to be an crime and obligate all other nations to collective action against the aggressor. This will be certainly difficult, but it is absolutely necessary. The risk of indifference is today incomparably greater than the risk of action!

Let us remember that it was exactly the silence of the great denomination that resulted in the loss of importance, the outflow of the faithful, and the emergence of new political religions that very soon turned out to be totalitarian tyrannies. Despite that, a large segment of well-known intellectuals and artists from the West supported them as an example of social justice, and willingly closed their eyes to the terror and unmitigated dictatorship of a small minority over a population of millions. The European elite evidently had not passed the examination on rational thinking.

There is also the question of whether, in the face of the obvious partiality of all religions, any of them has the right to interfere in politics; particularly in so important a subject as war and peace. Particularly in democratic countries, where religion is considered to be a private affair and any attempt to disturb the division between Church and state brings immediate and violent contest. Moreover, Christianity, as founded on divine revelation, is strongly convinced about possessing absolute truth, and has always justified war in defense of faith. And this makes doubtful the impartiality of judgments and sincere cooperation with other religions! One can therefore expect serious resistance to any correction of these age-old traditions! In addition, there is a certain contradiction here in presumptions, because such a task would require neutrality in local politics with parallel engagement in serious international conflicts. But since there is no other way out, let us look for positive arguments. I shall list them below:

1. Human nature. It is a paradox that today, in an epoch of triumphant relativism, logic and common sense alone are no longer sufficient. Only the touch of metaphysics can make us resign from narrow egoism, and force us to observe a simple mutual decency. The human being who has started to believe that he is merely a piece of matter and pitiful byproduct of aimless evolution is unable to honestly resign from selfish indifference to the needs of others. In order to overcome his own low status he is ready to accept any sect or political ideology that gives him a more stable point of reference – even at the price of his own rationality.

2. Absence of an alternative. Experience shows that officially atheistic regimes turned out to be belligerent, militaristic, and adverse to personal freedom; and therefore, incapable of carrying out their stated mission. All leftist revolutions started from demanding justice for the people and ended as dictatorships. This refers to the entire 20th century; to all continents, and all cultures. Every kind of Marxist "opium for masses" turned out to be highly destructive in all aspects of life.

3. Pragmatism. Despite all the mistakes committed, Christianity contributed to the emergence of the only civilization in agreement with the needs of modern humans. Moreover, it has endured hundreds of years of internal conflicts and philosophical dispute that made it gentle, tolerant, and willing to compromise

4. This is the only one religion demanding *"love for your neighbor"* and compassion for others as its principal message. *" (Matthew 22:37-40)"*

All these reasons may prove to be decisive, but in order to convince skeptics the arguments cannot any longer be supported by prophesy or revelation, but rather only by objective facts that explain reality and appeal to the intellect. Wars must stop to be a legal method of resolving conflicts; not because God wants it, but because it is (on the present stage of development) in conflict with our destination in the entirety of universal design. We must remember that we live in times when politicians and mass media may pronounce the most fantastical promises, but religion, paradoxically, is expected to provide sober and impartial analysis of reality.

It is not a question of changing canons of the faith, but of complementation of Christianity with a ***nonmaterialistic explanation of the reality*** that could be accepted by people today. If one wants to find a way to the hearts of 6 billion people who are not Christians, and who are either skeptics or followers of some other religions, he has to appeal to universal values build on solid theistic foundations consisting of two always-binding canons. First, the rational conviction about the existence of the Absolute as the creator and indispensable condition for the emergence of an orderly universe, and the second – the moral message brought to us by Jesus Christ. Together they will create the common, basic, worldwide basis that can be accepted by all religions and which will permit them to simultaneously continue their own traditions and beliefs. Each of them may uphold its own traditional for, but with the full understanding that it does not result from an ultimate truth, but from the civilization characteristic for this exact place, time, and specific phase of maturity.

This would call however for a change of certain, hitherto used, notions. Humanity, looked upon from the universal context, can no longer be considered an unintentional single incident (or an exceptional miracle), but rather as realization of the general idea of spiritual, intelligent beings. And the main aspiration of such being is no longer to be an obedient sheep of the Great Shepherd, but a mature, responsible coworker of the Absolute. The true "salvation" of humanity means now to liberate it from the constant prospect of self-destruction.

The basic problem is that man has never evolved into a selfless creature. Altruistic behavior is in fact just the opposite of what Darwinian evolution requires and may bring the end to evolutionary experiment! It is the last chance to notice that the famous *original sin* is no longer a consequence of minor disobedience committed in Eden, but as a result of our inherited greed and want of power that make us eliminate our own species. Humanity suffers from an inclination to overcome common sense and the natural instinct of survival in order to satisfy self-destructive, or rather species-destructive attitudes, which are the exact opposite to what is actually needed. We can clearly see that the present accumulation of science that precedes the development of civilization and of higher feelings decrease not increases, our chances to survive.

But how to solve this problem in a world full of different and so often antagonistic beliefs and interests? How to change behavior developed over long years of evolution? Answering this question needs much greater preparation than mine. Perhaps one of the ways could be establishing an international "moral rating agency", a worldwide organization called to evaluate the degree of danger hidden in the current foreign policy of particular countries. The method of persuasion should not be only the traditional appeal to the better part of human nature, but to the instinct of self-preservation. It must become clear that all solutions, apart from honest disarmament, are pernicious illusions. And ***none*** of the sides (whoever they will be) has the practical possibilities to prevent nuclear retaliation, and to avoid the subsequent death of tens of millions of people (also their own) from the blasts, radiation, and later break down of infrastructure. We must also realize that the part played by God is, in this case, restricted to giving us free will and intelligence; and, in the final effect, responsibility. So, there is no reason why our self-destructive behavior must always prevail over our intelligence and logic!

In order to survive, we must create a ***civilization of mutual trust*** without the present suspicions and fear of unexpected aggression. Considering this as the new challenge of Christianity complies with the requirements of the epoch, the recommendations of the Gospel, and common sense. The final goal is, of course, the introduction of a contemporary, world-wide *Pax Romana*; built not on legions, but on wisdom, compassionate hearts, and good will. This looks like unjustified optimism, but the present situation is so threatening that we must openly air such ideas for our salvation.

There is a bit of optimism in the fact that humanity has already shown a certain ability to form international organizations – starting from the Delphic Oracle, armistices at time of the Olympics, the League of Nations, the UN, and now the EU. This experience can be used now, when we face the possibility of mutual, ultimate peril. After all there is no doubt that today, at the beginning of the 21-st century, the world is a better and less cruel place than it was in the times of Octavian. And there is also no doubt that this change happened thanks to centuries long effort of all Christian Churches to introduce respect and empathy for another human beings.

It is certainly true that the division between church and state is the healthiest situation for both – the Church and the state. Men are naturally attracted to power; and when the Church, as an entity, assumes political power, it inevitably leans toward abuse of these possibilities. It can be avoided by independent, autonomous, nondenominational churches where the leadership is directly accountable to its members, and no one else. However practice shows that the division of Christianity into different denominations works to the advantage of success in international activity. The presence of many churches of various size and organization provides many examples to follow- from small private communities able to act efficiently and on their own initiative to the great worldwide organizations, like the Roman Catholic Church able to act on the international forum. The cooperation of such diverse types of attitudes, from folklore-like traditional images of saints, angels, full in legendary narrations to the dry, intellectual approach, clearly shows the vitality of Christianity and the enormous richness of its culture. It is like a great garden filled with trees, flowers, colors, and scents to choose and enjoy. An example of different character, tolerance and beauty.

Unfortunately, in the world's perspective we still see opposite cases; multiple attempts to combine government with divine authority and to declare that God wants us to die fighting in this or another "Holy War"!

Despite all these objections, Christianity still remains the only (albeit not world-wide) hope for saving humanity from itself. If this will not be done by the common effort of all denominations, other religions have even smaller chances. We cannot count on some happy accident or on some kind of miraculous external intervention, which (as experience shows) did not prevented the Bolshevik Revolution and the bloodbaths of two world wars. In addition the "progressive camp" does not offer great hopes, either. They traditionally promote peace, equality, and tolerance; but simultaneously introduce the principle of relativity that makes impossible their practical introduction. This has been repeatedly confirmed by completely free and unrestricted interpretation of liberal ideas. We have seen how often Marxist states built on the idea of freedom became totalitarian, capitalistic, nationalistic, and openly class-divided; or even became the property of the family of the ruling first secretary. This is, after all, the logical consequence of seeing the order of nature as "a happy coincidence" because it makes everything else accidental and relative. Any clear and permanent recognition between good and bad becomes so difficult that, in effect, it leads to the subordination of the public good to the interest of rulers.

Conclusion: Contemporary Europe is becoming less and less self-confident, but still represents a cultural paradigm that clearly exceeds its political position. It holds its standing only thanks to the inertia of its former reputation. But there is simply no other culture that could replace it now. Since every inertia must, sooner or later, exhaust itself, there will come a day when it will either recover, or become only a recollection of its former glory. If this will not be accomplished by Christianity, the greatest hope rests in logically justified theism and resulting universal morality. This work proposes a new form of Christianity founded on a picture of reality supported by a rationally explained order of the universe that seems to be closer to the truth than any other one.

Finale

The last question I want to ask is purely practical. How can we share these thoughts with others who think similarly? There are many ways, and one of them is to organize independent, private discussions comprised of a few intelligent people who reject ideological materialism, as well as uncritical faith. I have in mind those who know how to conduct orderly discussions about concrete subjects without unwanted digressions, to evaluate objectively consequent arguments, and marshal already-drawn conclusions. It would be great to attract a few scientists, particularly from physics and biology, familiar with the current state of knowledge. The principal goal of these assemblies would be to search for the logical, not accidental, structure of reality – and do it quietly; avoiding an atmosphere of sensation and exaggeration so characteristic of today's world. Having in mind the duty to leave the world better than we have found it, it could go together with some kind of philanthropic activity

But how to call these groups? Because a name should reflect intentions, I propose to call them: **"Affiliations of Rational Hope".** Perhaps, after some time, they would evolve into an intellectual movement of a wider range. It is too early to talk about their organizational form; but we can certainly find a few examples of well-organized, small communities providing a sense of belonging and friendship, along with the possibility of a free exchange of ideas.

I shall describe now the vital intellectual preconditions expected in these affiliations:

Elementary approval of the order of the world described in this work, but with full understanding that it is only an initial version which with the flow of time may change either under the influence of new ideas or because of the progress of the science.

Necessity of being aware that despite natural ambitions to find the *"definitive truth"* we will be able to achieve only the *"most probable"* point of view. And this in turn means agreement for resignation from considering our actual judgements as the ultimate and *"only truthful"*

Deliberate avoidance of direct involvement in any kind of actual political conflicts or in other fights for acquiring or maintaining power. However, independently of staying away from real politick, our general attitude shall be the support of democracy with all its attributes. As well as active, practical care for preserving harmony between the nature and civilization. Moreover, because the main location of our affiliations will be certainly democratic countries with strict division between state and religion.

Full approval of the fact that as a result of the replacement of faith by logical conviction and of ultimate truth by the most likely, there must be acceptance for remaining only an exclusive private affiliation that will never become a separate, popular religion.

But this type of compromise is still looked-for by large groups of people who are not able to find, against common sense, any authenticity in the present image of God and, for the same reason, cannot believe in the complete randomness and absurdity of the world and of our life on it. This is the reason why Affiliations of Rational Hope may play an important social function by providing a feeling of intellectual community for those who cannot find it elsewhere.

I realize that it will be difficult to transform these private activities into a popular movement since participation in it will require time and effort without promising any material gain. But, in exchange, this would offer an opportunity to rise above the noise and stress of everyday problems, and enlarge one's understanding of the world. Moreover, —it offers the opportunity to be in friendly and interesting company. And this – as everybody knows – has been always difficult; yet remains exceptionally precious!

Good luck
R.H.

Part two

General outline of notions for use of the followers of Affiliation of Rational Hope

The new form of Christianity presented below is the logical consequence of the obvious existence of the single, all-encompassing reality shaped by the cooperation of spirit and matter. This is the first, general outline of the proposal for a new type of Christianity which, I hope, will be approved by future participants of the Association of Rational Hope. I am not able to present here a complete project for "a new Reformation", but I believe that the aspects brought up here will serve to initiate further discussion.

My goal is **not** to replace the existing form of faith – let's call it the narrative – but to add a new one, in line with contemporary times. I still regard the main strands of this religion, as represented by Catholicism and the other great denominations, Protestant and Orthodox, as the most suitable for acceptance by their millions of followers and as still being capable of continuing and developing this civilization. The persuasive power of this narrative, one rich in varied components, has been confirmed by 2,000 years of practice and by the magnificent culture which it has helped to create. That is why the text below **is not** destined for people who are deeply and truly believing and who accept the official dogmas without serious reservation.

However, I see too much indifference and aggressive materialism not to realize that the influence of Christianity is systematically decreasing together with its impact on the fate of the world. Therefore, I believe that there is a need to present a new, more coherent vision, one which can attract many unbelievers and the indifferent who are nonetheless inclined to introduce a spiritual element to their personal lives. I consider the events described in the Gospels as real, but I give them a different interpretation. My whole reasoning is intended for those who are looking for rational arguments to return to the old concept of a higher order of being. And for those who are looking for a more rational explanation of the world.

The Christianity of Rational Hope is a new, successive attempt to tell the same ancient legend attained in a time when the Earth was perceived as the central, most important place in the universe and the scene of the struggle of sinful man with an almighty but just God. This legend has been enriched and developed by Judaism with the addition of many true historical facts. Christianity complemented it by new facts and located it in authentic place, time, and in ancient Mediterranean culture at the time of early Roman Empire.

Now has come a time when this legend cannot withstand confrontation with the new, scientific reality. The imagined, after a human pattern, Holy Family is not prepared to deal with the huge universe where our Earth is only one of billions of planets and perhaps one of many millions that are suitable for life. There is a need for adaptation of the presently obliging canon to actual circumstances and to such reality as we know it now – that is, at the beginning of 21-st century.

I shall try now to describe the doctrinal consequences which the presumptions suggested in this work may bring to the present form of Christianity. The text below presents in consecutive points new changes introduced into "a canon of convictions" treated as facts by adepts of the *Affiliation of rational hope* – if such a congregation will ever appear. My goal is not the criticism of what other people believe in, but merely an attempt to draw conclusions from the standpoint represented here.

The Old Testament, although always valid as a great work of religious literature, loses its meaning at the moment of accepting the only, single spiritual-material, reality – with the exception of these fragments that will remain in the DNA of European culture (e.g., the 10 commandments). This entails an automatic discharge from all the responsibilities that still obligate the followers of traditional Christianity. And accordingly, from the necessity of humanity's salvation from the consequences of *original sin* as committed by our first parents.

Fact 1: There is only one reality consisting of two, and only two elements: spirit and matter. The universe exists in a state of eternal movement and its evolution, as well as reincarnation, have a cosmic range regarding space and time.

Conclusion: There is no other "external" or "only spiritual" sphere of reality, where there is a place for heaven and hell, where God, the Angels and the Saints reside, and which, some day, will be governed by the "Kingdom of Heaven". This single reality contains, like on Earth, different spheres of spiritual advancement, accessible for their inhabitants according to their cognitive and emotional capabilities. Perhaps elsewhere in our universe there live billions of individuals possessing souls, and who create societies at a different level of spiritual development. It cannot be excluded that some of them possess physical and mental capabilities outweighing even the "heavenly" persons (like angels or devils) present in historical and present religions. But all of them live in the same space as we do, in the single existing reality, not in any "higher", external, or exclusive spiritual sphere.

Fact 2: The Absolute is the single necessary, everlasting, self-reliant and intellectually independent component of spiritual-material reality and the author of the idea of the entire organization of the universe in a state of constant evolution.

Conclusion: Consequently there is no, and it cannot be any contradiction between Him and rest of the world, just as there is no such contradiction between spirit and matter. Let us remember, however, that He is also the exception within the same reality because He is the only entity that exists outside of time. He changes His form from active to contemplative, depending on the state of particular universes that He creates. Being eternal He represents the natural opposite to nonexistence, and the reason for the recurring appearance of sequential, ever different and original universes.

Fact 3: Each human being possesses a soul, which independently and by its own effort ascends to the Absolute over the course of the long travel upward, ever developing during consecutive incarnations. The theatre for development of the soul is the entire universe. By way of a permanent process of transformation the soul approaches closer to the Absolute, gains better understanding of His intentions, and eventually joins Him at the last moment of existence of each of the next universes.

Conclusion: We are individuals and as such we are not subject to collective judgment and we do not accept shared responsibility for the errors committed in the past. Our souls will be verified separately and personally, primarily on the basis of our own actions and their consequences for other people and for the Nature understood as a harmonious opus of the Absolute. The chances for our future incarnation will also depend on our ability to make progress; whether we are leaving, by the end of our life, a better world than it was at its beginning. And if, while here, we have contributed (even to a small extent) to its improvement in any concrete way. This is in accord with our basic observation that mental states alone belong to the domain of the soul and become real only in co-operation with matter.

These criteria are more important than faith in the existence or non-existence of the Absolute because He is the basic condition of the existence of everything that is purposeful and meaningful. This relates also to the appearance of ourselves and of all that surrounds us. He is not *a jealous God,* because He has never been forced to compete with Baal or the Golden Calf. The effects of His presence, and especially of the order and the richness of nature, existed long before the advent of people who could believe it or not. Belief or unbelief are only subjective, personal characteristics of intelligent people and they work exclusively through them, acquiring meaning only when they affect human actions. In order to become a conscious participant in the attempt at the harmonious development of the Cosmos it is enough to be convinced that the Order of Nature is not accidental – and this belief is characteristic for all religions. The details are of course desirable, but of secondary importance. And thus arises the need to resign from the credo that repentance and faith in the voluntary suffering of Christ are enough to be saved (in our case, to deserve the next incarnation). Jesus does not assume liability of the people for possessing a soul and their own free will. This would be contrary not only to logic, but also to fundamental justice. Too easy and not fair toward those who leave behind some visible traces of their activity.

Fact 4. The pursuit of understanding God is inherited, natural and sincere for all creatures possessing a soul. However we humans will never achieve genuine knowledge of the Absolute because the human mind is not able to comprehend Him fully. Only by progressing upwards thru recurring reincarnations will we will get close enough to Him to perceive Him better.

Conclusion: Despite these limitations, we have the right to create His most likely images. We know that the Absolute is also made of spirit and matter but we don't know anything more. We suspect, however, that this is not organic matter. We reject His resemblance to humans, especially mentally, because if the human being was created like God, God must be like a human being. Considering how greedy we are and how fast we destroy the magnificently rich natural world, which has taken hundreds of thousands of years to emerge, the Earth created by a god similar to humans would have never had a chance to appear. And if so, it would become unsuited for life and/or quickly be destroyed.

Fact 5: Responsibility for maintaining the harmony of the world stems from the causes and effects of the decisions of particular persons, taken both on the personal and collective scale. The relationships between individuals and society are in the whole universe the same as we see in everyday life here – society **does not** bear legal responsibility for mistakes made by individuals. Blaming a whole community for an act committed in the past by an individual person is as unjust as individual responsibility for decisions accepted by the collective. The reward for positive cooperation in maintaining the harmony of the world is always individual, while the penalty for the common, deliberately negative or neutral, indifferent attitude applies to all concerned.

Conclusion: Accordingly, humanity has never been and never will be in need of salvation, comprehended as Jesus Christ accepting responsibility for our sins. Neither in exchange for sincere faith in Him as a voluntary victim or as compensation for some legendary disobedience committed by a particular person.

Fact 6. The idea of the salvation of humanity from the effects of Divine wrath for the disobedience of the first parents is a central issue of Christianity, always present at the heart of this religion. Our bad, selfish characteristics are still treated as a continuation of the events in Paradise, and thus we must work hard and then die instead of living forever and enjoying the eternal “dolce far niente”. The official abandonment of this version of events, and acceptance that our numerous defects are of a different origin will introduce an indescribable change of atmosphere, and above all the rejection of the guilty feeling imposed by the Church that permeates the entire emotional sphere of Christian civilization. It would take away unjustified anxiety about future disasters hanging over humanity. And with this will appear the possibility of taking over our own destiny. We no longer will have to expect Christ to judge and save us – we will regain power to influence our fate. This will restore a naturally justified optimism and joy in the fact that – despite our imperfections – to all of us and to everyone separately will return the happiness of being alive and taking part in the miracle of conscious existence.

Comparison of Jesus to "innocent Lamb", a victim sacrificed to God by ungrateful mankind, is offensive to Him, unnecessary remnant of an ancient, barbaric habit of killing the sacrificial animals in the hope of gain acquiesce of deity. If we treat His words pronounced during the Last Supper (*This is my body given for you...* Luke 22.19.) as metaphorical poetry in order to commemorate a moment, we will create a tradition of the shared eating of bread with wine, which may be the beginning of a beautiful symbol of solidarity and of memory. On the other hand, if we consider these words as literal information, we start to be aware of taking part in a collective eating of the body of an innocent victim we have killed and made to suffer for our own benefit. This may clearly suggest that Jesus has been sacrificed to God at the initiative of people who wanted to break free from the disproportionately large effects of an act of disobedience committed in the imaginary, legendary Garden of Eden by equally legendary first parents. Not to mention the natural opposition to eating the flesh of our own species as well as toward the tradition of human offerings, so alien to Judaism and to the whole Mediterranean culture. Fiction prevails here over common sense, pessimism over optimism, and gloom over the joy of life.

Moreover, the official interpretation of the Bible does not provide any logical cause-effect connection between the necessity of Jesus' death on the cross, and the disobedience of Eve. In addition, this former misbehavior is disproportionately small compared to the suffering of Jesus and even more to condemnation or the salvation of the world. But this obvious imbalance has never been acknowledge by the Church.

Besides, I do not see any reason, logical or even less emotional, to justify in such a way the real drama of the crucifixion of Christ! Even less rational seems to be a version of the voluntary sacrifice by the God-Son, to let (the consubstantial with him) God-Father free the whole of humanity from the old sin of disobedience to himself! As well in the requirement by the father for the martyrdom of his son for his own satisfaction and wounded ambition! From this perspective, the current concept of salvation, so important to Christianity, is unlikely both logically and emotionally. Fiction again prevails here over common sense, pessimism over optimism, and fear and gloom over the natural joy of life. All these are remnants of a mixture of fairy tale with tragic truth in the course of compromises concluded during the period of theological disputes in the early centuries of Christianity.

Conclusion: Salvation should **not** be comprehended as burdening Jesus Christ with responsibility for the bygone, legendary sins of humanity, but as the effort to direct further development of Western civilization in a gentle, less selfish and more friendly direction. For the collective, this meant the creation of a civilization favorable for harmonious existence, but for an individual this means the opportunity to achieve, by subsequent reincarnations, the highest possible degree of spirituality.

Fact 7: This situation would change dramatically when the place of the Biblical God-Father is taken by the Absolute – the Highest Awareness and Intelligence, the author of the concept of the universe in a state of evolution. People burdened by undeserved guilt would gain the possibility to change into optimistic, active contributors of the Absolute, who needs our help to perform tasks on a cosmic scale. Some of our problems will still remain, but their solution begins, in much larger degree, to depend first and foremost on ourselves.

The greatest dilemma of the human species, its truly "original sin" and the worst feature of our character is the gap between our morality and practices. The list of our faults is long: greed, hypocrisy, want of power, selfishness, cruelty, indifference to destruction and to the suffering of other forms of life – and this is only the beginning. We see clearly how quickly the amazing diversity of living forms that developed over millions of years of evolution is changing at first into monoculture and then into desert. The increasing efficiency of the tools of war threatens the existence of humanity itself, and it is not ruled out that sooner or later they will turn the Earth into a dead planet. All of this certainly carries us away from the harmony of being as intended by the Absolute.

That is why at a certain point in history we received a clear warning. At the beginning it was a seemingly insignificant event, but one which changed the character of the whole Roman empire and later the entire world. The man who did this was a young carpenter named Joshua, from a village called Nazareth, known to all of us as Jesus Christ. In compliance with the Gospel, at the age of 30 He experienced enlightenment from above and felt compelled to share it with others. Although He seems never to have written a single sentence, He masterfully employed the spoken word using parables and comparisons to illustrate episodes from everyday life. The main motive was the request for mutual kindness, decency and benevolence between people and the proclamation of a new (at this time) idea of social justice. The content of His sermons and the growing number of listeners and followers unsettled the religious establishment and became the reason for the conspiracy against Him and later for his undeserved judgment. They saw Him as a competitor because He claimed that by His life and teaching He represented the people before God and God before the people.

Conclusion: Jesus did not come to condemn us, but to push the further development of ours, the most dynamic civilization in a more kindly and morally responsible and direction. For the collective, this meant creating a culture conducive to the harmony of existence – and for the individual, the opportunity to achieve, by subsequent reincarnations, the highest possible degree of spirituality.

We cannot be saved by "the voluntary death" of Jesus because in fact he was tortured and murdered against His own will and had to share the same painful experiences as any other living creature. Before His death, He suffered all kinds of human wickedness that He wanted to warn us about: betrayal, scorn, mockery and hatred, cruelty, and finally disappointment. His death was a result of political intrigue that cynically drew on the Roman authorities' fear of riots in the province. Pilate preferred to convict an innocent man than to risk new troubles and having to apologize before the emperor. Jesus became a competition to the hierarchy because He claimed that by His life and teaching He represented God to us. He said many times that He did not proclaim His own ideas, but repeated a message from His father. In fact He could not be the "son of God", in the meaning of the son of the Absolute who, by definition, is so different and so much exceeds the level of all others living creatures that He never interrelates with them in any kind of family connections and may not be the father, mother, or son who interferes in the conflicts among creatures living at a lower level of existence.

But this is exactly He who enabled us to know the intentions of the Absolute to the extent that it is available to us. Only on this basis can one say that He was then coexistent with God. That is why the recognition of Jesus as not only a man, but the Personal Envoy of the Absolute, is also the closest to a valid understanding of His position and message. Therefore He will always remain and remembered as the founder of the religion of Christianity – whatever its form will be – even if His position will be perceived not as the Son of God, but only as the Messenger of the Absolute Message to humankind. What Jesus has really done is to have extended moral law, making it universal. It was not a continuation but the beginning of the new era. His words and His example will forever be the most important ones in all forms of this religion. He fundamentally widened the scope of the moral law and made it universal and always valid. This wasn't a continuation, but the beginning of a new era. The Christianity of Rational Hope will be then in the same situation as Islam and Buddhism, which are impossible to imagine without their founders – Muhammad and Buddha.

Fact 8: The introduction of these modifications means an indescribable improvement of the whole atmosphere that presently reigns in Christianity. Particularly important is the official rejection of the feeling of guilt permeating the entire emotional realm of this religion. This will remove the unjustified burden of an unpaid debt hanging over the entire humanity and replace it with a reasonable optimism and joy from the truth, that all of us together and each individual separately have received the gift of being alive and taking part in the miracle of conscious existence. We will also irrevocably get rid of the ever present horror of hell as a place of eternal suffering, whose existence is clearly opposite to the harmony of the world and to the notion of a loving, merciful God.

It would also mean the change of perspective from exclusively earthly to universal. In times when our horizon of thinking was restricted to the area of a flat Earth, which was thought to be the center of everything that exists, it was possible to imagine that it is governed by one unusual family consisting of several people remaining in extraordinary relationships (three of them are coequal). One can look for an analogy in the closely related Olympian Gods, but in each case we may see this as a creation of human minds that already for a long time has not fit the picture of the great universe revealed to us by physics and astronomy.

Conclusion: Together with the development of knowledge, human tasks and possibilities have changed significantly. It is not enough to carry out the simple order, undemanding of mental effort, for purely biological (*be fruitful and multiply to fill the Earth* ... Gen 2:28), which, by the way, has already been excessively fulfilled and currently starts to be dangerous. In spite of this, over the last two thousand years, thanks to our own energy, we have grown to become a serious candidate for the position of a responsible partner for the Absolute in the creation of global and cosmic reality, including already the entire solar system. The distant prospect offered by evolutionary reincarnation gives us a hope that working together with other thinking inhabitants of the Cosmos we will someday achieve unimagined spiritual and physical progress.

Fact 9: Such a kind of humanity has been under the special protection of Jesus Christ, who for us will always remain the Special Envoy of the Absolute and our personal friend and symbol of the embodiment of the Supreme Intelligence; someone who brought us closer to the Absolute and let us understand Him better. No longer a severe judge at the time of the Apocalypse, but the everyday close friend and counselor, constant – in the scale of duration of humanity-protector, advisor, and guardian of our fate, straightening ways of development of subsequent human civilizations. His life, pain, death, and resurrection are and will always remain a sign of understanding and solidarity between God and humanity. However, we know that thanks to Him and through Him the Absolute has descended to our level, pointed to us a new direction of growth and shown solidarity with our suffering.

The "second coming" of Jesus will **not** be a dramatic end of the world accompanied by Final Judgement! That would be contrary to the principle of individual evaluation required by rules of reincarnation. His second coming has already happened and it was His short appearance for a few days after His death (*in a short time you will no longer see me and a short time later you will see me again* J 16.16). The resurrection of Jesus Christ may be considered a real to the extent to which He has been remembered by the Apostles, that is by visions, meetings, and conversations. It will forever last as a symbolic revival of life giving us hope for the future incarnations on a higher spiritual level

This return, however, doesn't give the impression of a resumption of interrupted activity, but rather of a farewell visit. Note the fundamental change in the nature of the risen Jesus! This is no longer the young, energetic man who wants to change the world. Nor is this the rightful son of God who may use his power over the laws of nature to punish those guilty of betrayal and injustice and still continue His mission! Thus would have done the God of the Old Testament who burned down cities for much smaller offenses! The risen Jesus resembles rather an intellectual and inspirational teacher disappointed by what has happened to Him, a man who realized the impossibility of revolutionary human improvements! His return is limited to a few selected places and people and strictly private without a large audience and unnecessary decoration. His body also has become completely different – Jesus does not want to be touched (J-20. 17), passes through walls (J-20-19,26) and decides by whom to be recognized or not. (J. 21.4, 24.29).

He preserves the external form of His body, but the substance and the soul are already different – they are destined and ready for an extraterrestrial future. From the short conversation with Mary Magdalene one can guess that this is a transient state before the next incarnation. This is rather the short return, with the intention to prove to the people that Jesus was indeed the Messenger of God (Absolute) and that not everything must end with death. He also orders His disciples to carry on and independently pursue His mission, that is, to steer humanity's progress towards universal standards of goodness and truth. ("feed my sheep", Jan 21 -16,17, 18). You can see clearly that he is going to leave us alone so we can mature at our own time! In order to build a new faith we have to use all that He has left behind – what has been already said must suffice! And this is anyway too much for our comprehension. Who will believe in His teaching will deserve the next incarnation, and who does not, his soul will disappear without a trace.

However, in the days immediately after the death of Jesus, there was nobody who had grown to such a task intellectually. A someone who would gather His statements, and build upon them the concept of the new faith. But after a short time we again see an unexpected "intervention from outside" – that is, the sudden illumination of Saul, who later as Paul will give shape to the new religion – Christianity, together with the new interpretation of benevolence, love, and the ability to forgive.

It was Jesus who taught his disciples the prayer Our father, without fear that we all may start to believe that we are the sons (and daughters) of God. It was obvious that He was using a metaphor. The word “father” in this case means no more than “our loving guardian” and is used by all who turn to God for help. But this does not prove anything because it refers to the well-known experience of millions of praying people – especially in the case of war or during natural disasters – who have hope that God will spare them from the worst: suffering and death.

Some of His assertions indicate that, at least to some degree, He believed this way and hoped to get as much help as a son may expect from his father. For Jesus did not want to die, he wanted to live and act! This was confirmed by His words when he prayed in the garden of Gethsemane: “Father, if you want to, put away this cup from me; yet not my will, but thine” (L.22, 42). Though He repeated this prayer three times, God remained silent! Why? Perhaps He wanted Jesus' death as a sacrifice for the atonement of original sin? Or perhaps God simply did not exist? I am almost sure that Jesus, who certainly never doubted the existence of “God, the Father” understood this silence as undeserved rejection.

Silence to a call for help was certainly not the reaction expected from a loving father! If the so often cited: “God so loved the world, that he gave his only begotten son ...” (John 3.16) is (as the Church understands it) a valid description of things, then God was ready to sacrifice Jesus on the altar of “original sin” in order to adopt Him as son and equal counterpart, resigning from monotheism as the primary requirements of the creed! Both explanations are very unlikely because the whole tradition of Judaism indicates that the mere thought about altering the Divine hierarchy was blasphemous. This was accepted by the early Christian

Church and – by and large – has not changed to this day. This means that the phenomenon of recognizing Jesus as a new God happened much later and of course independently from Judaism. Looking from the current cosmological perspective, Jesus' real inspiration did not come from the legendary God of the Old Testament but from another source – the Absolute, the Highest Intelligence, and the only reason for the existence of the real, organized universe.

But then no such promises of rescue had been made. Being a man bequeathed with a free will and high intellect, Jesus was supposed to take care of himself. He realized this only at the last minutes of His life. That's why He shouted with disappointment: "my God, my God, why hast thou forsaken me!", (M.15.34). Was He at that moment in the depths of His heart convinced of being the son of God, and therefore also God? This we do not know, but it's very unlikely. It was not Greece where the relations of gods with humans were an entitled part of the Olympian life. The legend of the God of Israel was different and even when we assume that He represented the same, but historically earlier image of the Absolute, He certainly could not agree with such a humiliating situation. So since neither the potential son nor the father participated in the creation of this idea personally, it had to be the work of other participants, the later Fathers of the Faith. In order to establish the new role of Jesus one first had to create Christianity, this new, beautiful legend; and together with it the new magnificent civilization that still lasts and only now, after two thousand years of unparalleled success, has begun to look for new explanations and new narratives.

The conclusion about the death of Jesus is clear – it was not a voluntary sacrifice for humanity, but rather the outcome of events in Jerusalem. And if so, it could not have been intended as Redemption! Therefore, it does not save anyone but puts the strain on all humanity as guilty of the millions of those killed and tortured in history! There is no reason to think that in the case of Jesus' pain as an innocent victim there is any justified indifference or cruelty on the part of the executioners! Let us remember that His death, so far away in time and space, does not relieve any of us from our responsibility for the wrong deeds we personally commit against our neighbors and the harmony of the world.

Conclusion: Regardless of all the modifications here, and particularly despite the changed position of Jesus Christ from God incarnate to a human being inspired by God, He will always remain the most important figure in the history of humankind. He signifies a rare intervention into the life of people who have a soul and free will, showing them new prospects for development.

His coming was a rare exception in the essentially independent shaping of the history of intelligent species. If we really are not accidental pieces of living matter, but part of a larger, intended entirety, then the possibility of an occasional "intervention from the outside" seems to be likely and even obvious. After all, the general direction must be maintained.

There is no doubt that the effects of the activities of Jesus on Earth are impressive. Despite numerous setbacks, Christianity has changed for the better not only Europe, but also the rest of the world. And this change was launched by just three years of activity by an itinerant preacher, with no participation of the elites, organizations, or propaganda. Even if one may discuss some miracles done by Jesus, the results of his teaching are real and cannot be called into question. What is the conclusion? Let's stay with Christianity since it passed the practical exam of history and will pass all the next even after amendments and adaptations to modern realities.

Once again I repeat: the subject matter described in this book is not intended for believers, but for those non-believers who want to live in a sensible and orderly world. I'm not saying that what I have written here is a true description of our vast reality, but I think it is the most likely and therefore The Most Discernible Order of Being. Appreciation of these proposals does not require faith, but only conviction, which is an act of will and feelings – I believe because I want to believe! But conviction is an act of reason – I'm convinced about their correctness because there are numerous facts and their outlines can be seen through the veil separating me from inaccessible TRUTH!

Comment Here is an example of the difficulties in comprehending the official notion of salvation encountered by even the best motivated follower of Christianity, who tries to understand the logic of the official creed of faith:

In the ancient rites of sacrifice we have always the same three autonomous entities: a. A donor who asks for some favor from b. God, who in turn accepts the sacrifice of the donor. c. Finally, the victim itself, that is either agriculture product or animal or human. It is evident that living victims are always deprived of any choice and led by force to the place of execution.

The status of Jesus (as the victim) was exceptional because we assume that He was not just a man but also the Almighty God who could not be physically coerced – and this means that He had voluntarily agreed to death and suffering. The role of donor was played here by the entire humanity asking for forgiveness from its original sin, and from the related potential condemnation, of which it wanted to break free from. God was the God-Father (Yahve from the Old Testament), and the victim was his son, who at this time was fully human. However, simultaneously He remained also God because He was "consubstantial" with His father– whatever this term means.

The first question is whether humankind, being so subordinate to God the Father, could condemn his son (temporarily incarnated as a human) to torture and death against his will? The answer is a clear: "they could not!". Humanity must obey if it doesn't want to be punished by a flood or some other disaster; disobedience is consider to be the greatest sin. Therefore, we have to believe that either Jesus himself had chosen death on the cross and later resurrection in order to free humanity from the effects of its former sin of disobedience to His father; or He was selected by God as a victim that will free humanity from the sin of disobedience to himself! But since Jesus was all the time consubstantial with his God, the Father, by condemning Jesus, he had chosen himself to placate himself! We do not know why He should do so instead of simply forgetting about the whole affair. In any case, the logical and emotional motivation of such a choice as well as the sequence of cause and effect are inconclusive here.

One can of course say that the fault of humanity is not in fact found in the story with the apple, but rather in the nasty traits of our character. But then again this is not any human's fault because he was created by God *in our image, in our likeness* (Gen.2.26). This means that the human being is "genetically burdened" not through his own fault – he received his inclinations without his own participation. So what would be the sense of God denouncing his own son to a painful death in order to free himself from responsibility for his own "design errors"? And how can someone who is omniscient and omnipotent make any mistakes? But this is a separate question!

Part three

Polemics

Introduction

The weakness of an atheist's arguments is that instead of reality, they refer to the mental state of the interlocutor. Instead of asking "Does God really exist?" atheists ask "Why did humans invent God?". The factual state is never discussed because a negative answer is already included in the presumptions. An atheist believes that God does not exist and all that is left is to demonstrate the defectiveness of the mind and character of those who think differently. He assumes beforehand that he is dealing with a product of pure fantasy or of backwardness. By resigning from objective exploration of the external world, he reduces the whole problem to psychology. Because this attitude is contrary to the principle of impartiality, all pretensions of atheism to represent science are unjustified.

Secular humanism presumes to give the human being the highest intellect, but at the same time denies him freedom to use it. Assuming in advance that God – or any other spiritual phenomena – does not exist, secular humanists refuse to admit that the mind has *the ability to speculate that allowing it to free itself from the illusionary picture presented by senses.* Since we know that animals – so close to us biologically – do not have abilities for abstract thinking, what entitles us to assume that we are not subject to similar limitations in relation to a higher intelligence.

The dog does hear music and see a picture, but it does not notice or understand their composition. This does not mean however that these notions and corresponding spiritual reality do not exist. Similarly we know that human senses do not cover the whole of reality – not even just the physical, why do we claim that all that we cannot notice or understand does not exist? So, how can we claim that we are on the highest possible sensual and intellectual level and why do we assign to ourselves much higher status that we are entitled to? If we consider ourselves to be an accidental and meaningless form of matter we cease to be "someone" and became merely a "something" ! How then can a "thing" pretend to such decisive opinions?

The principal purpose of the text below is to present the most popular arguments for and against the existence of a higher intelligent force responsible for the development of the world. I am not trying to prove the existence of this or another God, but rather only the presence of a rational order of the world and of our existence as its result and a logical part. Experience tells us that all that is orderly is intentional and all that is intentional has its beginning in a conscious mind. This marks the limit of our comprehension of the world. All that is above it is only a supposition. However this is still much more than blind faith or equally blind disbelief because it lets us speculate what the purpose and meaning of our own existence may be.

The set of theses and antitheses below presents a brief attempt to answer the most popular atheistic arguments, ones constantly repeated in all "progressive" publications. To remind the eternal validity of this problem I have used a traditional, medieval form of presenting two opposite arguments. I hope that this short review proves that commonly used description of materialism as the only one correct and scientific viewpoint that is rational and worthy of contemporary man, is completely unjustified arrogance. Familiarity with an abbreviated counter opinion will allow the reader to adopt an independent standpoint and wrest free from fashionable prejudices.

Each argument against (materialistic) is answered by an argument for (theistic). Replies are kept in a neutral spirit, without reference to any particular religion. No reference to revelations or to mystical experiences because from an atheistic point of view they cannot be considered worth discussing. The language used will allow everyone to understand the arguments used by both sides.

Ideas

1. "Is there any conscious creative force responsible for the order of the world?"

Materialist: "No, there is not!"

Nature does not provide any evidence that evolutionary changes could be caused by some kind of intelligent and purposefully acting factors. There have never been observed physical laws which act particularly favorably toward the hitherto direction of the universe's development. It is accepted as true that the presently known physical laws are quite sufficient to claim that nature alone can produce more and more complex, living and purposefully acting organisms. They are a purely material byproduct of a chain of mutational accidents and of natural selection. Being such, they are neither an aim in themselves, nor a medium leading to other intended aims.

Theist: "Yes, there is such a force! Its presence is confirmed by the hitherto history of cosmic evolution! When we consider that the universe is indeed developing in a clearly defined direction, the probability that it was designed for some describable aim is much higher than that emerged accidentally and without any reason.

a. In the world we live in a majority of the changes of the state of matter are results of previous decisions taken by living, intelligent beings. The scope and kind of these changes are in direct proportion to the degree of spiritual advancement (in this case of intelligence and motivation) of those who make these decisions. And this in turn depends on their position on the evolutionary ladder. But since the Earth constitutes an integral part of the common universe, there is no reason why the same hierarchy of causes and results shall not be obligatory all over the rest of it.

b. It is self-evident that there is hierarchy of physical and spiritual advancement of living beings. The order of the human world is visibly more complex, and therefore higher, than the order of the animal world. There is no reason to think that we are on the highest possible level of spirituality and intelligence. The fact that a snail does not believe in the existence of humans does not prove that we do not exist.

c. Presuming the existence of a single, common spiritual-material reality where the status of living beings depends on the proportion between spirit and matter, it seems self-evident that it must have two extreme opposite poles – namely, the highest, most complex form of spirit and the lowest, simplest form of matter. On one side we have then the simplest passive and thoughtless substance and on the other active Highest Intelligence, able to design the universe. That is someone whom we call God.

d. The **c**laim that certain fragment of dead matter – in this case, some accidentally emergent forms of protein – suddenly began to replicate themselves in order to produce living forms incomparably more complex than the initial product, is an obvious reversal of commonly observed relations that happen between causes and effects and between objects and subjects. The appearance of life and intelligence – the two most important events in the history of cosmos – have been reduced here to a marginal incident and portrayed as a byproduct of the independent action of dead matter, which has been elevated to the rank of a thinking person. This is conscious ignoring of the existence of a clear hierarchy of causes and effects that decide the changes of the existing environment – both spiritual and material. The whole of nature points to a dependence between level of mental development and ability to undertake decisions and to predict their results. This is clear, everyday evidence of dominance of spirit over the matter.

e. The theory of the natural selection of the best fitted refers exclusively to living organisms and therefore it does not explain why universal evolution was so clearly directional ***before*** the appearance of life. There is not the slightest reason why accidental physical forces, might, acting consequently and for such a long time (that is, from the emergence of the universe till now) change the initial chaos into higher organized forms of matter. And even less likely to create a living and thinking person. We do not know even one example where an accident has caused such a long-lasting, upward- directional evolutionary process leading to the emergence of entirely new, previously non-existing qualities of quite different character

Conclusion: *The visible directionality of evolution clearly indicates that the probability of the universe's intentional design is much higher that its accidental self-e*

2: Is faith in God consistent with science?

Materialist: "No, it is inconsistent!"

The hypothesis of the existence of God cannot be scientifically verified. Religions originated as an explanation of natural phenomena and reaction to the fear of death. Thus, the origin and function of religion are subjective and purely pragmatic. Science clearly shown that everything that exists is a part of nature, comprehended as a purely material mechanism acting independently and without any intervention from outside. The universe, including ourselves, together with our thoughts and feelings, can be explained by mutual interaction of material particles moving accordingly to physical laws in response to changing conditions. The very existence of nature so understood is unintentional, accidental, and aimless. Summing up, in the scientific explanation of the world there is no place for God, and therefore He does not exist.

Theist: "It's the other way around! Science points towards the existence of a Highest Intelligence!"

a. Let us start with the separation of two notions: faith and confidence. The first implies a collection of religious commands and restrictions based on descriptions of revelations and other happenings very often contradictory to everyday experience and scientific observation. It is true that faith so understood cannot be scientifically verified and this remark refers to most of the present religions. This situation changes diametrically, however, when we replace such faith with confidence based on rational reasoning showing that reality is orderly, organized, and purposeful. And as such it cannot be accidental.

b. Contemporary science cannot resolve the problem of the existence or non-existence of God because it is exclusively occupied by examination of matter and by answering the questions *how* matter is built and *how* it behaves under given circumstances. But this is not enough to answer whether nature created itself or has been created. Scientists by definition do not ask *why* something happens and what might be the possible aim of an activity, and therefore is unable to deliver even one proof that God does not exists. However, along with the progress of knowledge, reality appears to be so orderly and mutually coordinated and the conditions of emergence of life so narrowly defined that regarding it as the result of an accident cannot be seriously considered.

Therefore the claim that the living world and human spirituality (understood as self-consciousness and the ability to think and to feel) are the result of a *series of accidents and fortunate mistakes,* has become even less likely. One cannot commit a mistake without having an aim or a plan of intended action. However, along with better knowledge about reality we see more clearly the outline of such a plan suggests the presence of a mind that is able to conceive it.

c. It is true that none of the reasons for the appearance and hitherto development of the universe can be either confirmed or falsified by experiments designed and performed in laboratories. But it is also true that if the world were chaotic, science could never happen. In such a world it would be impossible to confirm observations, draw conclusions, and systematize the growth of knowledge. What is more, because the human mind is not only a part of the existing order but also its result would be equally chaotic. How then could we have any confidence in the credibility of scientific observations and in the logic of conclusions? But the fact that we can learn about the laws of the nature, successfully reconstruct the sequence of previous events, and use this knowledge to build credible models testifies that our thoughts are quite coherent. Thus, not only the order of nature but also the existence of minds able to examine it confirms the logic of the entirety and therefore the existence of the spiritual part of reality.

d. It is a matter of fact that all observations confirm the apparent direction of universal evolution leading from simple to complex, from lifeless to living, and from thoughtless to thinking. This direction has not been changed since the beginning of the universe.

Another fact is that the progress of cosmic complexity started long **before** the appearance of life and therefore

could not be a result of natural selection. It must be some other, unknown to us mechanism, serving as the method of realization of the same goal. If so, this mechanism must be designed by the same author, but for different stage of the universal evolution.

Conclusion: *Science confirms the directionality and purposefulness of universal evolution and consequently the existence of a self-aware creative force.*

3. Is the notion of God coherent?

Materialist: "No. It is incoherent!"

Since the existence of God is neither obvious nor commonly perceived, His explicit perception is beyond human possibilities. The traditional description of God as immaterial, but at the same time, a living, active, and creative person is incoherent. Similarly, His other features do not always agree with each other, and do not find equivalence in reality. A thing that cannot be coherently and logically defined does not exist.

Theist: "Yes, the notion of God is coherent"

a. It is true that a truthful and objective definition of God exceeds our intellectual capability. All we can afford is an approximation supported by two premises. The first presumes that the order of the nature is not spontaneous, but designed and therefore requires the existence of a designer. The second, that the character of creation reflects the character of its creator. Such argument does not provide unquestionable certainty, but refers to real, verifiable human experience, giving it attributes of truth. Apart from this, we do have on our side the intuitive, internal conviction about the existence of the natural order of the world. And this must have a rationally explainable reason, one that provides the previous reasoning with additional coherency.

b. Traditional images of God were based on revelations; that is, on information given to certain chosen people by divine personages. But these, of course, cannot be impartially proved. What is more, His image built on revelations contains conflicting attributes; which indeed makes it incoherent. It is impossible to reconcile His immateriality with life, His omnipresence with being a concrete person located in a particular place, and His unlimited goodness with injustices resulting from the nature of life. Especially since the connection of omnipotence with faultlessness makes Him fully responsible for all the wrong of the world. However, these inconsistencies do not testify that He is absent, but only that the image of a higher personality cannot be brought down to the level of a lower mind.

c. Then again, we will find ourselves a bit closer to the truth once we reject historical images and recognize God (or the Absolute) as a natural, necessary, intellectual component of reality. In this case there is no reason why He could not remain an individual, self-conscious person and, at the same time, represent (always and everywhere) the idea of the order of the universe. Or acquire such a form of life (unknown to us) that can last eternally. Even if this new picture remained only a general outline, it will become more contemporary and, in effect, more likely than the traditional one. Since (so far) all His images have reflected possibilities of the human mind on a certain level of development, we have the right to think that our present knowledge allows us to build a new image closer to the truth than the one from the time of Ptolemy. And hope that along with spiritual and material progress this reflection will become more truthful and closer to His real character. There is of course no rule that refers to "contemporary" or "traditional" matters when it comes to God. One's concept of God is more truthful than others when it contains more verifiable facts. Consequently the later conceived image should be more likely that the former one, but only when it is in better agreement with actual understanding of reality.

I realize that such abstract thinking cannot replace religion with its metaphysics, tradition, color, esthetics, and ceremonies; but it is certainly closer to the truth than pseudo-scientific atheism or uncritical faith. It will help us to be more tolerant about traditional religious forms that proclaim the same truth, but in another, more poetic way. And allow us to remain within a circle of the magnificent civilization built with the participation of Christianity.

d. The impressive progress of knowledge made in the last century promoted the exclusively materialistic model as the only one possible. However the latest discoveries of cosmology changed this picture. New telescopes show a complex and mutually-synchronized universe, which can no longer be explained by the independent and accidental action of lifeless and thoughtless matter. It requires the presence of an intellectual component of nature. The concept of exclusively material evolution as an exclusive cause of the hitherto development of the universe is coherent only under condition that it is considered as a consciously-designed enterprise. Without the previously conceived universe as a logically developing entirety it would be impossible to explain the close coordination of such factors as the favorable initial state and of natural laws followed by consecutive beneficial fluctuations. All of this excludes an accident as the cause of the present state of the universe. The notion of "Accidental Providence" is essentially inconsistent.

Conclusion: *All religions are truthful in their fundamental statement that some Supreme, Creative Force exists; but they are at the same time false when they claim that they know exactly who or* what it is. *Nevertheless, the bare fact of acknowledging its existence permits us to change the image of the universe from incidental, unexplained phenomenon to an ingeniously planned enterprise; and our present, "modern" status from an unnecessary, soulless biological mechanism into one of thinking co-creators of the universe. From now on we are no longer responsible for the sins of our legendary ancestors, but for our present behavior toward other people and to the nature. This metamorphosis is certainly worth tolerating all that divides us from those who respect the same ideas, but give them a different form. And to close our eyes on things we are not able to believe, and to concentrate on those which contain the same moral principles.*

4: Do immaterial things exist?

Materialist: "No, they do not."

All that exists consists of matter (that is of particles, forces, fields of energy, etc.) formed and moving in accordance with the laws of nature. The examination of matter can explain all possible phenomena. Consequently, all that existed or exists – no matter where or when – is material. It means that the entire universe can be explain by modern physics

Theist: "Yes, they do!"

The reality we live in consists of things material and immaterial. About the latter, the most important is life and its derivatives – that is, conscience, thoughts, ideas, and feelings. It is true that to become real these derivatives need a material brain, but in their essence they remain immaterial and therefore spiritual. In spite of this they cause real results. Without a share in the spiritual sphere we would not exist as intelligent beings, nor talk and act sensibly, or create art and science. Analogously, we ourselves could not emerge without previous, clearly directional cosmic evolution which prepared conditions that allowed for the realization (here on the planet Earth) of our particular case of the formerly conceived, general concept of a person endowed by the soul. Thus, we owe the existence of the universe as well as our own selves to the intellectual initiative and will to act of some mind that was able to conceive and change its ideas into material form. Experience shows that surrounding us human reality works in the same way. Unfortunately, science does not admit the fact that matter remains continually passive and has never (apart from fairy tales) provided an example of any kind of an independent intellectual initiative. Most scientists deny the existence of a spiritual sphere of reality as separate and distinct from material reality – an attitude that brings everything that exists to the lowest, purely physical common denominator.

Conclusion: *While it is true that each of these two realities depends on the other, (physical hunger can cause*

a willful change in behavior; and mental stress can cause physical ailments), both of them are separate and neither reality has derived or evolved from the other.

5. Is there any truth apart of science?

Materialist: "No there is not! Only scientific opinions are credible!"

In the exclusively material world the only true and credible statements are scientific judgments that can be experimentally confirmed. No other criteria of truth exist. All other judgments are relative and either subjective or motivated by the interest of those who proclaim them.

Theist: "Yes, there is! Science is concerned with only the material fragment of the real world! Examination of matter does not provide information about events taking place in the spiritual sphere and does not explain such basic problems as the reason for the appearance of the universe or its meaning and destiny". It is also worth remembering that many scientific judgments cannot be experimentally confirmed. The materialists, like most of us, are influenced by political ideology, but often are just not sincere enough to admit it.

a. The classical definition of truth is the conformity of a with the current state of a given reality. Therefore, the "ultimate truth" ("absolute" or "universal") is a judgment based on complete and objective knowledge about the whole universe including all, former and present, physical and spiritual events. Analogically, truth about a given thing or event requires the same kind of knowledge about this thing. Since all knowledge depends on the sensory, mental, and spiritual possibilities of an observer, the ultimate truth can be known only to someone whose possibilities are endless – that is to the Absolute. All others are limited to merely subjective and fragmentary truth because they are constrained by their natural abilities characteristic for the whole species and to a given individual. The judgments of all creatures living anywhere in the universe are only as truthful as they are close to the ultimate truth. The best indicator of truthfulness is how they work when practically applied to the conditions of the real world. If a species or a person is able to survive in the environment in which it has to live, this means that it is also able to recognize at least as much of a truth about this environment as was necessary. Despite the fact that our perception is to a high degree subjective, the basic facts are mostly in accordance with reality. A car accident can be remembered differently, but cannot be perceived as a storm on the sea. If the differences are too big, either the observation was inadequate or the observer indolent or inaccurate. These remarks refer also to moral values that are felt or perceived by common sense and intuition.

b. Observation alone does not create scientific theories. Researchers postulate the presumably existing laws of nature and results of their application in given circumstances. Later they verify these presumptions through specially designed experiments. Thus, so called, "scientific truth" does not result only and exclusively from examination of matter, but depends also on the state of mind of those who plan the experiment and interpret its outcome. Since physical laws could be reduced to the statement: "*if x then y*" they represent only a fragmentary truth, a contribution to the eventual construction of the most probable model of reality. The required mental work belongs however to the domain of the soul, whose character does not depend on a given experiment. Matter makes only half of the machinery that moves the revolving stage of life. The remaining part belongs to the incomparably more complex spiritual sphere. The statement "if x, then y" already implies spiritual input, since drawing a conclusion ("y") is also a mental, spiritual exercise. Depending upon the mindset of the scientist, the experiments might be constructed in an entirely different way; and display an quite different outcome. We are not merely subjects but also co-authors of reality, because we constantly add our concepts to the drama in which we play our parts.

c. Scientific judgments change along with progress of science and therefore are almost never ultimate. History of science contains lot of statements that turned out to be false.

d. In order to be objective, scientific statements must be articulated in the third person. But in our everyday experience we think and take decisions in the first person. I can experience life only as ***"I"***, exactly this, not any other thinking person. This experience is purely personal and does not belong to presently binding definition of scientific notions. If only scientific statements were truthful then our personal life would be false. But this is contrary with experience because the very fact that we have succeeded in surviving proves that at least part of what we do is in agreement with the nature of things. Our lives are certainly real, not illusory, but our bodies exist objectively and independently from our consciousness. The perception of ours surroundings is always subjective and as such does not fit into the scientific definition of truth. If all statements expressed in the first person, practical and theoretical were false, then all our judgments, including scientific, would also be false.

We could not then be responsible for our thoughts and their results, be able change our surrounding, build civilizations, or invent anything. But there is no doubt that we do so! The fact that we have been doing it so long (before the beginning of experimental science) proves that it is not the only single source of knowledge.

e. The claim that only scientific statements are truthful is based on the belief that the human mind is able to make correct observations and to draw from that proper conclusions. But all that can be examined by physical experiments (even by instruments incomparably more sensitive that human senses) is, finally, perceived by these imperfect human senses and interpreted by our naturally limited minds. Even judgments confirmed experimentally always are to some degree subjective, due to limitations characteristic for individuals and the whole species. We simply do not know how much our way of thinking is shaped by our biology. And we will never find it out without comparing our opinions (including scientific ones) with an opinion formulated by some other intelligent species.

Conclusion: *Scientific judgments are assumed by the persons who utter them to be objective and true. However, the presumption of objectivity and truth involves subjective reasoning. Thus, even if such reasoning is confirmed by additional experiments, the final conclusion depends to some degree on an individual interpretation – that is, on the intellect and emotions of its author. This means that some scien-*

tific judgements (like definitions of laws of physics) may be truthful (water always consists of two particles of hydrogen and one of oxygen), but the way of thinking leading to this conclusion is always individual and subjective and does not have to represent the ultimate truth.

6.Revelation, myth, or truth?

Materialist: "Revelations are merely products of human imagination".

The majority of religions, including Christianity, are founded on revelations –that is, on descriptions of personal contacts of gods (or their representatives) with certain chosen people. These revelations are considered to be undisputable facts despite being based on impossible-to-prove verbal transmissions and their written versions. Belief in their authenticity is, in its essence, merely faith in the reliability of those who claim that they were subjected to it and/or those who repeat it. Regarding revelations as facts is entirely unjustified. Despite the fact they are supported by castes of priests acting in their own interest.

Theist: "The lack of the credibility of Revelations does not testify that the world is purely material or that God does not exist".

The essential motive of religion and science is the same – an attempt to understand the world and our place in it. Both are trying to answer its aim, meaning, and way of doing. Christianity for ages provided an explanation in accordance with the reigning spirit of the époque. Theology tried to reconcile faith in revelations with the current state of knowledge, but the growing difference between the religious and scientific explanation of the world made this impossible. Today, the doctrinal demand of faith in "Holy Scriptures" as literal truth contributes to the widespread abandonment of religion and the laicization of culture.

Such literary interpretation justifies religious intolerance, imposing one's faith on others as *God's will*, and advocating death on the battlefield as the best way to paradise. There are uncountable (historical and contemporary) examples of using this argument by extreme religious fanatics and by cynical politicians. In the face of today's universal access to the internet, as well as to modern armaments, this kind of manipulation of minds brings mass calamities and may destroy civilization. History proves that such a danger may come from the side of some religions as well as from political ideologies. In this aspect nothing has changed, we still see multiple examples of indoctrination and coercion used to control the thoughts and lives of individuals and societies.

It must to be stressed however, that impossible to verify revelations do not prove that materialism is right, but merely shows a deep disparity between the traditional and modern state of minds. Presently, the existence of God can be more convincingly concluded from the scientific picture of reality. Moreover, resignation from revelations as the source of information does not change the fundamental message of Christianity. The command to behave decently toward other people and to nature will always be valid. Even the most eager materialist cannot find in this anything contrary to present level of knowledge or common sense.

Conclusion: *The impossibility of verifying revelations does not change the fact that the presence of some* *kind of a higher, beneficial, and constructive intelligence becomes indispensable in explaining the logic and order of the universe. Science constantly delivers new evidence that the world is sensible, purposeful, and rationally organized. And we are its intended and necessary component.*

7. Can science solve all the problems of humanity?

Materialist: Yes, it can!

Throughout the last three-hundred years experimental science has contributed to an unbelievable increase of knowledge and well-being. Poverty and hunger have been reduced, health improved, epidemics eliminated and human life prolonged. Mass production and efficient distribution has increased the general comfort of everyday life above the former level of privileged classes. All this brought about an equalization of opportunities, the spread of democracy, education, and human rights. We begin to grasp the cosmos and have reached the stars not only metaphorically, but also in reality. In light of these achievements the superiority of the scientific viewpoint over the religious is inarguable.

Theist: Yes, all of this is true, but let us remember that atheism is not a condition of technological progress – one does not have anything to do with the other. The 19-th century was still Christian, but brought greater progress than the 20-th! And besides, have we become better or more happy because of that? Are we closer to each other, more friendly, or at least less lonely? Or perhaps gentler, more tolerant, or possibly less cruel?

Not at all! We feel divided, deserted, and disappointed as never before. In developed countries an average household consists of one person only, the family understood as a community made of parents and children slowly disappears, depression, drugs, and alcoholism are common. We still hate, wage wars, and kill each other in masses, with indifference and cruelty. The same inventions that improve our life serve as tools for universal indoctrination, the control of individuals, and as instruments of war – for more than half of century we have lived in the shadow of atomic war and the threat of total annihilation!

Materialism brought to its logical conclusion leads first to egoism, next to hedonism – and finally to nihilism. The motto *If there is no God, everything is allowed!* has attracted a lot of followers! Fortunately not everybody is a materialist and even those who are very rarely draw this conclusion. The approval of materialism as the foundation of culture is in collision with common sense and our intuitive comprehension of the world. What is more, practice confirms that over the past 50 years of Europe's laicization brought clearly visible negative biological and civilization consequences. Throughout this time the number of births has fallen by about half and the number of marriages has been systematically shrinking, European societies have become older and as a result less healthy and physically neglected. Confirmation of these facts can be found in any statistical yearbooks. It is of course true that the Earth is already overpopulated, but stabilization cannot be achieved by the voluntarily dying out of some groups and excessive multiplication of others.

But is this a fault of science? Not at all! Rather of those who agreed to make humanity a complementation of science and in consequence accepted materialism as their undisputable faith. But what is obligatory in science becomes an obstacle in philosophy because it does not allow us to ask the most fundamental questions. Once we agree to become exclusively material beings we lose our soul and free will. Without them we are no longer independent human beings, but only temporary things determined by accidental fluctuations of matter. No longer men or women but merely a passing phenomenon, with no aim and meaning. Without humans endowed with an individual soul the whole of humanity has become meaningless. Can we imagine the psychology of computers, even of those most advanced ?.

If it is true that the human race emerged by accident and we do not have a soul, we should be motivated exclusively by the sole imperative of survival and procreation. But it's the other way around! Because the soul is indeed the indispensable component of our personality, the majority of us are still able to behave decently and act with good intentions, sometimes contrary to our own interest. And because of that, there is still a hope that someday we will make the world better than it is now.

Summing up, conversion to materialism turned out to be fatal. We have lost hope and together with it freedom, dignity, and the meaning of existence. And in addition any expectations of future life! What is worse, we are not capable of inventing anything that could replace the soul, because as *purely material objects* we are not allowed to exceed the laws of physics. And these do not anticipate a soul.

But if we are indeed only a material item why we do not enjoy this role or feel well and comfortably? From where comes the ever-so-prevalent feeling of insecurity, loneliness and of helplessness? Would not be better to reclaim our former status and again become humans? Perhaps it is worth resigning from absolute freedom and irresponsibility and chose to take part in building a better world? To agree that **not everything** is relative and that beauty, goodness and truth, even if not fully reachable, still exist! How to stop being a thing defenselessly thrown into the black abyss of the cosmos and again become an independent part of a greater entirety?

But how to do it? How to harmonize physics with metaphysics? With all reverence for science, we should not allow it to enter domains which are beyond its reach. Materialism (as ideology) does not result from knowledge about matter, but from its narrowly understood political interpretation. This or another structure of the atom does not testify that the world appeared by accident or that God does not exist. If we look at it as a reasonable component of a greater, logical entirety it starts to point to something quite contrary. The best way to understand this new perspective is the close cooperation between science and philosophy, or even with religion, impartial and without presupposition. It will let us keep on with Christianity, but without forcing ourselves to believe in things that are unbelievable. However, do not let us slight those who want to stay behind tradition. They also have their own truth that is perhaps beyond our comprehension. It is more reasonable to preserve old culture with its all beauty than to believe in "good" or "bad" energy or in other occultist, commercial tricks.

Conclusion: *Science as a method of exploring the world is occupied exclusively with the matter and considers human being as accidentally-emerged material product. This is at odds with the true state of affairs because human being represents spiritual- material unity. As a person endowed by the soul, he or she is able to get out beyond purely biological needs and open his or her mind towards search for scientific, moral and aesthetical truth. It is therefore obvious that so comprehended science alone cannot build a civilization which could satisfy all needs of the complex human personality.*

8. Can the progress of science permit humanity to take over the role of God and become the creator of itself?

Materialist: "Yes it can." Continual accumulation of knowledge will allow for unlimited self-improvement of the human race, not only in the physical, but also in the intellectual sense.

1. According to trans-humanism, contemporary man represents a transitional state between the previous animal form and a future *perfect man.* Progress of science lets him become a self-creator of his own body and mind. He will decide about his health, intelligence, and memory and the length of his life. He will be able to pass from the real to the virtual world and to feel desired emotions. New technologies will permit him to replace the present human form with a new kind of mechanism free from any biological necessities. This entails the emergence of quite a new type of thinking beings. They will be at first *"post humans"* (or rather "supermen"), later a kind of a mixture between robot and human being, and finally a living robot. From the materialistic point of view human status will change only in the technological sense. The present, accidentally appearing, fully material biological object will be replaced by self-designed, equally material entity with quite different physical and mental attributes. The latest discoveries clearly suggest that the era of accidental development is coming to an end. The position which has been so far assigned to a fictional God will be taken over by the fully developed human brain working in constant cooperation with a computer. It opens before humanity new excellent perspectives!

Theist: "No, the human being cannot become creator of himself! The claims of the materialist are completely unjustified fantasies taken from science fiction novels and movies, combined with Marxist faith in shaping human nature by means of social and biological engineering. Human imagination and self-creativity, similarly as that of all others living beings, are limited by the range of innate physical and mental possibilities and hitherto practical experiences. This makes it impossible to predict and to design in advance a completely new, previously unknown task.

Trans-humanism is primarily a political movement, a combination of materialism and traditional humanism – two outlooks that deny the existence of God putting in His place the human being. It is a continuation of former attempts to produce a *new man*, a kind of *superman*, physically perfect and ideologically faithful. This time not by education but by direct physical intervention. The task is *to accelerate the evolution of the intelligent life*. Transhumanists hope that new technologies will bring about far reaching exchange of particular parts of the body, including the brain. This would not be (as so far) rationally justified replacement of non-working organs and treatment of genetic shortcomings, but direct encroaching upon the spiritual sphere – that is, thoughts and feelings. They talk about the connection of a computer's memory with the human's brain, the use of brain waves, *transfer of a mind*, biotechnology, nanotechnology, and other methods of this kind.

There is however no clear definition of a final task of this enterprise, nor of a permissible range of physical and mental changes. Nobody talks about new moral principles or asks whether we will become gentler than we are now or rather if we will hate each other even more. Will we respect at least a basic decency or try to exploit and deceive each other even more ruthlessly? Contrary to historical experience they presume that *human nature* is *inherently good and* will always prevail – even when we cease to be humans. We are dealing here with a new totalitarian vision where (according to Marxist principles) the *progressive* minority will decide the fate of the rest of humanity.

Nobody seems to care that the possible realization of these ideas must ultimately give rise to two different species. On the one hand will be improved (physically and mentally) *post-humans* – and on the other, those who will either remain in the present form or will be degraded lower. Any kind of exchange between these two groups – physical and mental – will end. This will bring a permanent division into a privileged minority and subjected masses. The introduction of genetically conditioned traits will exclude any modifications of a society so designed – whether voluntary or revolutionary. The ruling class will finally achieve full security by becoming not only stronger, but significantly wiser.

This means that application of this kind of "electronic eugenics" must, as all former attempts of similar kind (Nazi and communists), end in total disaster. The idea itself contains a basic logical contradiction; the range of imagination cannot surpass the range of hitherto known experiences. No living creature, including people, is capable of imagining own life otherwise than the same, but somehow improved. This refers to thoughts as well as emotions. A snail cannot visualize itself as a dog, with its intuition and lively feelings, and dog cannot think about itself as a human being with its ability for abstract thinking and creativity. In the final account, the enthusiastic descriptions of an expected happiness do not extend beyond the improvement of the present state of affairs. It turns out that human beings are not able to imagine anything more than they know from experience: better health, longer life, faster vehicles, more sex and food, telepathy instead of telephones, etc., etc. This makes it impossible to design one's own future differently. Such a design is basically similar form, though of a higher quality.

Let us also remember that every invention always has two sides – good and bad. Mechanical agriculture increases yields, but degrades the environment; airplanes make travel faster, but are used to destroy cities; nuclear energy produces electricity but also atomic bombs. It is worth noticing that the expected advantages are usually personal and instant, but real results unanticipated, widespread, and long-lasting. Even more so if the planned action does not concern passive matter but our active mind, a sphere that is almost unknown. Sometimes trivial and rather primitive political or religious indoctrination may trigger a total contempt for life – one's own or of others. What tragic consequences might result from inserting into the brain a "hate chip" or other, similar implement. Especially dangerous when there are no clearly established goals, ethical standards, or moral borders set for the intended pursuit.

Despite this, there is no doubt that the possibility of the physical modification of the brain will be used to achieve all possible goals – liberal or totalitarian. Either to reduce differences between classes, races, nations, and even men and women – or the reverse: to reinforce the feeling of distinction. In any case, by introducing a standardization of thinking we will lose our individual personalities and with them the perspective of further spiritual development. This will lead us to the lower, collective style status (on the scale of order of beings), and eventually to mentality similar to ants and bees.

Conclusion: *Everything indicates that attempts to accelerate or to revert the principle of self-development of the human species may end in its total destruction. Natural stages of spiritual advance cannot be so easily omitted. Voluntary resignation from free will and from our own effort for the sake of electronic programs, makes us, as a species, resign from reincarnation and in consequence from further individual existence. And from taking part in the creation of the universe.*

2. Secular God or the greatest social engineering in history of civilization

Throughout the history of mankind, civil power has attempted to equate itself with spiritual authority. In the ancient Roman Empire, for example, the republic eventually devolved into an autocratic form ruled by "divine" emperors who were to be worshiped. The organized Church has likewise attempted to replace secular government. Thus, the marriage of the throne and the church has been believed by both sides to be necessary. In the case of Christianity it was regarded obligatory from Constantine the Great till the French Revolution; and ceased to be in force with the emergence of the United States, the first modern democracy with a clear separation of the church and state. At the same time, rapid development of towns and growth of bureaucracies around the globe resulted in gradual increase of the extent of control of society.

Presently, at the beginning of the 21st century, citizens of all countries are subjected to strict supervision, and are identified by a myriad of numbers relating to their personal life, finances, property and functions in society. While this information enables the smooth functioning of administrations in both democratic and authoritative countries, it serves also to control and supervise the population in order to maintain power. There are numerous examples in many of the secular Marxist states of the 20th century.

Each of these secular states sought to create the overarching authority of the party leader; establishing an justification for the coercive obedience required to believe in a promised, but never-quite-attained, bright future. Paradoxically, the elimination of religion needed replacement by an atheistic equivalent of the Christian God: the secular version of an expected "kingdom of heaven". But how could such a materialistic, secular god take over the role of the God of Christianity? It turned out that while the "replacement god" was seemingly similar, it was, in fact, quite different.

The god of atheists, like the God of Christians, must also be omniscient and almighty. But since a secular god cannot govern an individual *inwardly*, it must dedicate itself to governing every *outward*, practical, and operational detail of its citizens' lifestyles. At the beginning of the 21st century the advancement of electronic technology and computer science provided the ability to identify the face of anyone who is within the governmental realm. This is accomplished through the use of hundreds of thousands of cameras feeding information into a huge database available to numerous government agencies. It is this accurate and objective knowledge that gives the system's owner the opportunity to interpret and assess the behavior of each observed individual. In addition, it provides the opportunity for immediate intervention in the case of disobedience to the rules. Combined with absolute civil and military power, this system deprives citizens of their freedom of choice and makes them completely defenseless before the government.

However, the greatest difference between the God of Christianity and its secular electronic equivalent is seen in terms of feelings and morality, and in the government's attitude towards individuals. The Christian God is compassionate and loving to the world He has created, is inclined to forgive, and is always righteous and impartial in His judgments. The "god of government", however, is by definition subjective; being programmed to always take the side of those who are loyal and dedicated to the currently ruling power.

Despite the millennium-old accusation that Christianity suppresses freedom of thought, materialists have willingly subjected themselves to total and absolute intellectual slavery to a secular ideology. Instead of a loving, forgiving, and unchanging God, they now face a pitiless, thoughtless, and lifeless electronic "machine", which controls them and rewards or punishes them according to continually-changing programs written by other people. Not surprisingly, the new "humanistic" religion has borrowed many of the external forms of organized Christianity. Modern socialistic "liturgies" use similar scenery: Processions with portraits of leaders, crowds passionately singing songs, and masses exhibiting enthusiastic devotion for ideological religion. The secret police has taken over the role of inquisition, with its prisons and denunciations. Heaven has, of course, been abandoned; but hell has found its equivalent in the form of poverty, fear, persecution and concentration camps.

Let us to illustrate how this new religion will look like in the largest communist country, that is the People's Republic of China. Please find below a brief description of present state of affairs. Most of information comes from Wikipedia and other commonly available publications.

The New Social Credit System in China

The best example of the helplessness of humanity in changing its natural, inherited character is presently seen in China. Its Social Credit System and will prove to be the largest attempt, in the history of civilization, to eliminate spiritual independence and remodel the human's soul. It is the first premeditated attempt to eliminate spiritual independence of human species. It is happening before our eyes, here and now. At the same time, we see clear evidence how a new technology may be used to satisfy the desire of secular human government to be worshiped In this case, the goal of this initiative is to acquire absolute power over the minds and bodies of more than a billion people.

System SCS is an official project of China's Government to ensure total control over the society. It is being tested now, and the Chinese agency Xinhua has announced the launch of its trial version with the participation of volunteers. After its installation the government will know everything about all citizens: what they eat, where they live and even what they do and say. Their actions will be observed and their words recorded throughout their entire life. This vision will someday become an everyday reality for all Chinese citizens.

For years the Chinese authorities have collected and stored the voices, the facial biometric data and the DNA of all China's inhabitants. Every monetary transaction by a citizen requires him to show his identification; and do so under the constant surveillance of a dense network of cameras and sensors. All of this information is continuously gathered on the government's servers by the most powerful Chinese companies from the IT industry.

By controlling the data from a citizen's payment card and compulsory presentation of identity, the system can follow what and where do you buy. Control of Internet will show what a citizen watches and writes. Due to a network of cameras on streets, face recognition software, and geo-

smartphones, authorities will know where any citizen is, and with whom he has met. This information will be further supplemented by constant examination of one's life as revealed by personal acquaintances, Internet contacts, and associates at work.

Every person, based on what he does or says, will be evaluated using a point system of scoring. The higher the point value of a given person on this scale, the more "trusted" and "reliable" (submissive and unresistant) he or she will be in eyes of the government. Citizens who score highly will be rewarded with more favorable treatment when obtaining loans or making substantial purchases. They will also find more favorable treatment when traveling, especially if traveling abroad. (A "trusted" citizen is more likely to return to the motherland and cannot be "seduced" by Western values.) Citizens with low scores may expect penalties such as prohibition to eat at nice restaurants, attend theatres or purchase tickets to special events. They may lose the right to travel abroad; and may even have their access to the internet limited.

More than this, a citizen's ranking will affect his ability to get a good education or find a good job. Not only will a citizen be screened by a potential employer; he will find that some career fields (as well as educational opportunities to prepare him for those fields) are closed to him if he is considered "unreliable Obviously, such an assessment will impact the enjoyment of life on a personal level, including the selection of a marriage partner.

Only government will have authority to decide what raises or lowers the score; and by doing so be able to give political meaning to every sphere of private activity. In consciously shaping the common and personal values, they will manipulate future reactions and behavior every individual.

One may predict that, as in the worse times of Stalinism, people will compare their own rating with other people and denounce each other to authorities in order to improve their own odds. But with China, the scale of the whole enterprise is this time significantly larger. In the Soviet Union under Stalin the ruling communist party-destroyed a total class of its citizens: one hundred million farmers. Under pressure of hunger and repressions, they were turned into employees of large state-owned ranches. China's plans today relate to the entire nation – one and a half billion people! Let us hope that the "partially capitalistic" communism in today's China is more sensible than it was at the time of the "cultural revolution".

But even so, "private lives" will cease; being destroyed by ever-present awareness of continuously being watched and the helplessness of knowing one's life can hinge at any moment on an impersonal and subjective rating system. Even in the privileged class no one will feel "proud and free". Fear will become a common national traits. With the loss of free will in every area of life, the health of a human soul is lost. Individual spiritual progress in the experiences of life will be considered too risky. In the emergence of modern civil society in China, it is difficult to imagine even honest, public discussion about any issue; not to mention the activity of any opposition.

I want to stress here that lack of resistance shown by the continental population of China to the introduction of SCS does not derive, (as some maintain,) from historical or cultural traditions, but from modern totalitarian thinking that stems from Maoism, Bolshevism and Hitlerism. The best evidence of this are massive demonstrations of the inhabitants of Hong Kong against changes attempted by the present communist government. Experiencing 60 years of life under a democracy was enough to mobilize Hong Kong's population to organize resistance to attempts by communists to bring the island under the legal system of the rest of China.

The universe

9. Accident or intention?

Materialist: "The cause of the appearance of the universe is purely material and its existence purely accidental and aimless".

We do not know the cause of the appearance and development of the universe, but we do have all reasons to think that it is the result of the laws of nature only. From its very beginning the universe has existed in the form of purely material cosmic evolution, proceeding from *down to up* – that is, from basic components to complete entities, from simple to complex, from lifeless to living and from thoughtless to thinking. The direction of this development was (and still is) determined by at least three accidental causes: a). advantageous initial state. b). particularly fortunate set of physical laws which spontaneously emerged in the first moments of existence. c). favorable fluctuations.

The fact that all these factors were unintended and accidental relates respectively to the whole course of evolution.

Consequently, all consecutive phases of the evolution were and still are unintended and do not lead to any clearly described task.

Theist: The universe has appeared as a result of an intentional, conscious, mental activity. For all that is real is the outcome of the execution of an idea conceived by a previously existing mind.

The above materialistic explanation is incoherent because on the one hand it attests that directional evolutionary development takes place from the first moment of evolution till now, and on the other still claims that it is accidental and aimless. But what is rational and directed ***cannot*** be at the same time irrational and accidental. The claim that nature is able (independently and on its own initiative) to use lifeless matter in order to bring the universe to its present state and create living, complex, rationally acting beings is statistically unlikely, intuitively false, and impossible to prove. It is also contrary to experience and to the historically confirmed sequence of causes and results.

Much more probable is that universal evolution is progressing in accordance with deliberately established initial conditions, a closely outlined set of natural laws, and under constant supervision. The orderly sequence of events suggests that the growth of complexity and appearance of the new qualities are ***not*** a result of an accidental, self-determining, unjustified action of matter, but the effect of consciously applied method. Steady direction of development of the universe from its very beginning to this day, confirms this assumption. It allows us to carry out the following reasoning founded (as much as the entire theory of evolution) on conclusions about the past drawn from the observation and interpretation of the present.

1. We know from experience that every rational action is a result of thoughts produced by a mind conscious of its intentions.

2. Science maintains that all over the universe the same logic and the same natural laws reign. If this is true, then all sensible material changes are always, everywhere, and in all scales of magnitude produced by previous decisions taken by an intelligent mind. Therefore the intentions of this mind can be guessed from examinations of previous history of cosmos and from effects they have brought so far.

3. Consequently, appearance and development of the universe must also be the result of the realization of an idea by the conscious use of physical laws by a previously existing mind. Certain share of accidents is here only a complementary, foreseen in advance element of technology that does not alter the general concept. This makes possible the adaptation of consecutive stages of development to local condition of a given planet, without serious alternation of its general course which points to a systematic increase of complexity and the emergence of new, immaterial qualities. The most important of them is life. It makes possible the emergence and development of all remaining spiritual qualities, such as consciousness, intelligence, free will, ability to experience emotions, etc. Their appearance ***cannot*** be explained by the exclusive action of natural laws and by the growth of complexity alone.

Conclusion: *The fundamental fault of materialists is an attempt to combine successful scientific studies with magical beliefs, and assign attributes of living persons to lifeless objects. So far, it has been never observed that accidental combinations of simple, material elements, acting only by themselves and without participation of an intelligence and energy from outside, produced a complex living organism, acting purposefully. The fact that a building has been built of various building materials does not support the claim that those same materials had started (at their own initiative) a string of events, which accidentally produced a house, fully equipped and ready to live in. Why then is this type of reasoning acceptable in regard to phenomena incomparably more complicated?*

10. Humanity – a success or a mistake?

Materialist: The human being cannot be the work of God because as a species humans show features which lead to self - destruction.

If God were omnipotent and omniscient He could foresee the results of His action. It might be expected that human beings, whose life depends on a food chain based on mutual devouring of living organisms, must possess all complementary features, and among them aggression and indifference to the suffering of species serving as nutrition. Combination of these inherited traits with the highest, (on the planet), intelligence and inventiveness had to, sooner or later, give human beings total control over the rest of the living world. And together with this the possibility of ruthless exploitation and destruction of the complex organisms found in nature – and finally of themselves. The prediction of such a course of events was from the beginning within the human (and even more, within the divine) range of prediction. To prevent this possibility, human beings, (as dominant species) shall be always equipped with a mechanism ensuring that the moral development will outpace the intellectual one. But this is not the case. Moral objections do not make people resign from brutal exploitation of nature or from constant improvement of military technology. All previous wars proved the dominance of instinct of survival over decency and common sense. And this may finally bring the total destruction of life on Earth.

Deduction: *The imperfection of humanity testifies that it emerged due to an accident rather than being conceived by a compassionate, all-knowing, intelligent mind.*

Theist: This conclusion would be right but only when all presently existing forms of life have emerged solely on the Earth as a single event, the only one in history of the cosmos.

All this starts to look differently, however, if somewhere, in the universe exists life and develops by method of evolution, but with some share of an accident. In that case, humanity becomes one of many examples of a great cosmic experiment – the realization of an idea of the being who possesses a soul. But this does not mean that humanity and every other intelligent species must survive! The collective survival of humanity similarly as reincarnation of individuals, requires specific traits of character and mind. Moreover, accidental factors also decide which species would understand its role to develop its intellectual and moral potential soon enough to overcome instincts to kill while fighting for territory. Let us remember that one can achieve the required spiritual perfection only in result of multiple, positive selection. In order to pass this test we have to overcome difficulties typical for *thinking animals* on our present stage of development.

Fortunately, not all has been lost in our battle for existence. We have seen how in the last century wars and revolutions had almost destroyed Europe. But we have seen also its efficient reconstruction and realization of the marvelous concept of European Union as an assurance of cooperation and peace on the continent. Even if temporary crises sometimes happen, any internal wars within once united Europe became impossible and some form of federation will sooner or later emerge. Similar tendencies are also seen all over the world. The costs may be higher than expected, but we are mature enough to pay them.

Conclusion: *Despite all temporary obstructions and difficulties, universal evolution still remains a consciously designed method leading toward the highest accessible perfection of the world. And homo sapiens, the only creature on the Earth possessing the earthly soul. Our future as humans leads way up through consecutive reincarnations to more and more excellent physical and spiritual forms that will allow us to become the co-authors of the future development of the universe. Per aspera ad astra !*

11. One universe or many?

Materialist: "The emergence of any environment friendly to life could happened in "our" universe because it is only one out of an uncountable

number of other universes where it was impossible. Only the existence of a great number of other, various universes justifies the possibility of such an improbable accident."

The fact that the universe we live in is ruled by physical laws favorable to the appearance of life is an exceptional and unusual good fortune. It was possible because our universe is only a one, single exception among many other universes, which are ruled by natural laws hostile to life. This has happened in accordance with the rule that in the case of an endless number of accidents going on in an endless number of places throughout unlimited lengths of time all possible accidents must occur.

Theist: "The hypothesis of the existence of an endless number of other universes is nothing more than a desperate attempt to solve one statistically impossible concept by replacing it by another, even less realistic and impossible to verify."

The claim that natural forces had created an unlimited number of collaterally existing universes and the presumption that we know what kind of physical laws there are and, what is more, drawing out of this such fantastic conclusions is logically false, statistically unlikely, impossible to prove, and contrary to experience. Therefore it does not have the character of a scientific judgment.

In the place of the proverbial ape which by hitting the keys of a computer for an adequately long time would write all Shakespeare's works, we have here billions of writing apes – that is, hypothetically existing universes - out of which only one was lucky. This equals the relocation of the same reasoning on the higher level of abstraction and lower level of probability. Why lower? Because we at least know that this first ape exists, is alive and able to press the keys. But we do not know whether any other universes exist and what kind of natural laws are there. Moreover, dead matter (wherever it is) always remains lifeless, passive, and does not contain any possibilities for independent, and even less for any purposeful action. And this rule is binding independently of lengths of time and the amount of matter involved.

If we will ever produce a living being possessing a mind and a certain range of freedom it will never happen by accident but by our initiative – that is, by the effort of living and intelligent persons. Analogously, in the case of the entire cosmos the initiative must belong to the Absolute – whoever He is! All attempts to reverse this sequence are completely unjustifiable.

Even if the hypothesis of a "multiverse" were true it would not prove the accidental origin of our universe. One may as well maintain that these assumed universes make together a certain purposefully organized entirety acting in accordance with some general concept. That they serve as laboratories to check what conditions are required to create life! Universal evolution would then change into "multi-universal" and become incomparably more complex and we would find ourselves once again in "the best possible universe". In the final account, the fantastic vision of many universes brings us back to the same problem we were trying to escape from, but on a significantly greater scale. If the Earth rests on four elephants which stand on sixteen turtles – what the hell do these turtles stand on?

The Human being

12. The Human being – rationale or byproduct?

Materialist: The human being is only an accidental byproduct of aimless evolution.

The discovery that the Earth is not the center of the universe, but only one of millions of planets in one of billions of galaxies testifies that the picture of humans as the aim of creation is false. Thus, the appearance of life and of thinking beings **is not** one of the goals of the existence of the universe, but only a long chain of happy accidents.

Theist: "The Human being is a deliberately planned element of the universe"

The change of the Earth's status from the center of the universe to one of many planets does not lower its significance as the site of the life. It's rather the reverse, because this fact allows us to conclude that universal evolution has spawned life in many other regions of the cosmos. If it turned out that the same laws of nature acting in similar conditions yielded the same results, then we are dealing with an intention rather than an accident.

The more we emphasize our unimportance and irrelevance the more we do need some steady point of reference, one common for the entire universe that would justify our existence. That is why atheism as a reaction to the discovery of our marginal place is precisely the opposite of what we actually need. The more we lower our status and try to descend to the position of animals moved by simple instincts, the more we become them. And this makes us less prepared to bear responsibility for the world we live in, and helpless before the forces of nature. Especially those we are subjected to. By putting man in the place of God we will more easily submit to our intrinsic egoism, neglect our duties, and finally destroy ourselves. This would be an obvious, but unfortunately belated proof of our mistake.

Conclusion: *The sooner we acknowledge the rationality of the universe and our responsibility for our part of it, the greater the chances we have to save ourselves as individuals and the whole species.*

13. The human – a spiritual person or merely a biological mechanism? Does human life have any meaning?

Materialist: "The human being is a purely material biological mechanism and his life is aimless and pointless!"

a. This aimlessness and insignificance of the material world passes on to the human species. Particular individuals are merely biological mechanisms driven by the instinct to survive and preserve their species. Apart from this, the objectives of their lives do not have any meaning beyond temporary existence. All human civilizations have originated as a method of survival, are provisional and will finally disappear without a trace.

b. Thoughts and feelings are products of an entirely material brain, which has been proved by the close ties of mental and corporeal states. Consequently, they should not be called spiritual because their origin is purely material. The human soul comprehended as an individual, personal, and spiritual entity independent from the body does not exist. Its idea is only a product of imagination produced under the pressure of the uncertainty of existence and fear of death. Diversification of understanding and emotional sensitivity among various species does not come from possession or absence of the soul, but from differences among particular organisms. Their abilities to think and to perform independent conscious activities are the result of evolutionary growth of material complexity. Summing up, human individuals are (in the qualitative sense) nothing more than an accidentally emerged material substance.

Theist: Human beings possess a soul and the meaning of their life depends on cooperation with the Absolute in building a more perfect universe and developing their own spiritual potential.

a. It is true that mental and physical states are mutually dependent. However, this dependence is not always identical, but variable and individual, closely connected with the stage of development and character of a given living being. And this differs it from purely physical dependence in chemistry or mechanics.

b. Physical apparatus of the brain is indeed necessary for the appearance of thoughts and consciousness. But these do not have the basic characteristics of matter and cannot be explained in purely biological categories. They are a direct product of the mind, which does not belong to the material sphere.

c. There is no doubt that certain animals show abilities to comprehend and to feel similarly as human beings. This is clear evidence that evolution systematically leads toward spiritual development preceding the emergence of the independent human soul. Together with it we cross proportional step between spirit and matter and we rise to the next qualitative level. The human being becomes *a person* for whom the spiritual sphere overcame the material. This means a fundamental change in the perception of reality. Thoughts and ideas became a decisive factor, motivations are no longer instigated solely by instincts, and personal intelligence starts to decide how to behave in complex, spiritual –material reality. The "potential soul" is changing into the "active (or rational) soul" – the only one component of the universe possessing possibilities to think independently and to adapt the environment to his needs.

d Mental states and thoughts do not have physical traits of matter and in purely material meaning do not exist. But they become real by the mediations of living beings who have a soul. They are perceived subjectively and directly only by the persons who experience them. Because they are expressed only in the first person (*I think* and *I feel*), they do not fit the present, obligatory definition of scientific judgments which are expressed impersonally in the third person.

The fact that these abilities appear together with evolutionary development does not explain why the transformation of dead matter may lead to the emergence of phenomena of a quite different character. There is no physical equivalent of consciousness or any specific threshold of complexity dividing the dead from living. It cannot be explained by selection of the fittest because there are species that do pretty well without self-consciousness so comprehended. It cannot be explored and described by methods used to research purely physical phenomena. One can rather assume that their appearance at a certain moment of evolution is an actualization of potential possibilities hidden in the cooperation of spirit and matter, in accordance with the plan of universal development.

e. The logical organization and consequent development of the universe find their equivalent in the activity of living, intelligent beings. There are at least three reasons for their existence. First is cooperation with the Absolute in further development of the universe, the second their own life enhanced by thoughts and feelings, and third the creation of new ideas and their materialization. All of them upgrade reality by introducing new forms and contents. Human life is not only a senseless vegetation, but makes an important and sensible component of the entire cosmos. The existence and development of the human soul are indispensable parts of the concept of universal evolution. There is a great probability that they will be continued by the method of reincarnation intended as a road leading to higher forms of spirituality.

Conclusion: *The Human being, similarly as all other intelligent beings, represents the only one of the examples of embodiments of an idea of a person possessing a soul, and as such is one of the principal components of the concept of the universe*

14. Do non-relative moral values exist?

Materialist: "No, they do not exist".

In the course of the evolutionary quest for survival, the human species developed abilities to live in groups and this in turn brought about the formulation of rules of behavior regulating relations between individuals and society. Thus, moral values are offshoots of the organization of society and therefore an entirely human creation. As such they are relative and depend on the level of civilization and on the current interests of groups and individuals. "Natural law", understood as having its source apart from (or above) the human world, does not exist.

Theist: "Yes, they do exist"

Morality arises from the necessity to maintain the harmony of the world required to protect life and further spiritual development. It is not a *sensu stricto* division into good and bad, but it expresses the same meaning in a wider sense. Such a notion of morality provides the foundation for "natural law" coming from observation and rational interpretation of objectively existing reality. It reflects accumulated, practical knowledge about the working of reality and therefore provides the foundation for all other particular laws. Its main message demanding mutual decency in human relations and toward all living nature is binding always and everywhere, intuitively felt, rationally justified, and confirmed by experience.

The notion of morality and its interpretation is accessible only for those who possess the ability to understand abstract ideas – that is, only for those who have a soul. This applies to relations among physically existing living beings, but in essence it belongs to the immaterial world of thoughts and emotions – that is, to the spiritual part of reality. If the universe is indeed a logically designed organism advancing toward an increase of spirituality, it must contain more harmonious elements than chaotic, because its further evolution is possible only under the condition that harmony will ***always*** prevail over chaos. This harmonious universe remains in its deepest sense "decent and reasonable", not because we are terrified by the alternative, but because it is the ultimate condition for its further existence. From this point of view the distinction between good and bad comes from what is or is not favorable for life and further spiritual growth. The ability for intuitive recognition between right and wrong does not change the fact that the human being is neither able to know the required range of truth nor to proclaim completely objective judgments. Therefore, granting him ultimate moral authority may result in destruction of the natural, both spiritual and biological, harmony – and in consequence, in the predominance of bad over good.

Conclusion: *The universe designed by the Highest Intelligence must be in its deepest essence good because every other one could not exist and even less to perform its assignments.*

15. Can atheism become the ideological foundation of a successfully developing society?

Materialist: "Of course it can!"

Religion is not able to solve the problems of modern society. Rather the reverse, it is opposite to the progress of science and development of democracy! Experience proves that the religious mentality is contradictory to the freedom of thought and even more to the personal freedom of citizens.

Theist: "No it cannot!"

History proves that all civilizations developed in symbiosis with some religion and none of them survived the fall or a change of this original faith into another one. This refers to the ancient world as well as to the contemporary one. Roman civilization felt together with the Olympic Gods and was restored in quite a different form under the influence of Christianity. Similar phenomena can be seen all over the world. The leaving of one's own religion always brings either the adoption of a foreign faith or the introduction of an equally strange political doctrine. It is true that in the history of Europe were times when the official religious viewpoint was enforced by state power, but this situation belongs already to distant past. Paradoxically, this system has been restored everywhere, where atheism became a part of the obligatory ideology. The experience of the last hundred years confirms this – both communism and national socialism (and lastly postmodernism) rejected religion in order to gain total control over the minds and freedom of citizens. This is a clear warning about the possible future.

Conclusion: *I can only repeat once more: either Christianity will be able to overcome the present crisis, or it will be replaced by another faith and another culture. Tertium non datur!*

16. Theodicy

Materialist: "If good, loving people God really existed, He would have created a world without suffering, death, and other evils, and would not permit all the injustice and suffering that has accompanied life from its very beginning"

The notion of God as someone who is omnipotent and at the same time loves humanity is, in the light of historical experience, clearly incoherent. If such a God really existed He would create different kind of life, without the food chain forcing living beings to devour each other, fight for their own territory, and to inflict suffering on other similar beings. He would also not let us be to so indifferent and cruel to our brothers. The present state of affairs clearly testifies that God does not exist and His image is unjustified fantasy!

Theist. "The existence of God, comprehended as an intelligent and personal, necessary component of reality does not determine the presence or absence of evil! It is either an unavoidable requirement for the emergence of life on the planet Earth or an effect of conscious human action! The last one depends only on us and so we can blame only ourselves alone!"

a. One does not have to be particularly smart to notice that this atheistic argumentation contains a principal fault because it consists of two parts that are logically incompatible. Firstly, the opposite statement – that only a perfect world without suffering would confirm God's existence – is illogical. The fact that the world has been intentionally designed does not impose conditions on the project. And even less that its presumptive designer has a duty to like and protect us or do anything to help us. And secondly, such a demand is nothing more than sheer, unjustified arrogance. For who gave us the right to impose any conditions on someone who is so much higher than we are? There were no initial negotiations and nobody promised us anything! We did not agree to be born only on the condition that everything would be easy and pleasant!

b. But there are yet other reasons why our demands are only superficially justifiable. First, the universe in order to exists has to be harmonious – that is, also rational and just. And the natural world is exactly like that. Only we humans have received a mind and free will that let us distort this harmony. Our accusations come mainly from the fact that we want (against common sense) to think about God as a person obliged to correct our mistakes. We do not remember that the role of the Absolute in human wrongdoing is limited to including us in the plan of creation and giving us intelligence, free will, and conscience – thus also the innate ability to recognize good and bad. Without them, we would be as innocent as the rest of nature and equally irresponsible.

c. There are of course natural disasters like earthquakes, tsunamis, and epidemics – but we cannot hold the Absolute responsible for them because they happen in accordance with physical laws and with the rule of limited randomness. They were anticipated in the general plan of evolution. They are also a source of suffering, but at the same time one of the conditions for development. Without limited randomness natural selection would be impossible. They make up one of the components of the mechanism of evolution and as such are beyond moral categories. We have been equipped with intelligence to prevent them and we do this quite well – we live longer, eliminate diseases, build dams, and to feed the great human masses. There is no reason that someone else should do it for us. Even less because it would require either change of the design's presumptions or exceptional, temporary suspension of natural laws.

d. If we then complain that there is too much evil in the world, we cannot blame anybody but ourselves. It is not God's responsibility that the human world is no better than humans themselves. It is unfair to burden the Absolute with liability for giving us free will – and with it the potential to do wrong. Before we start doing this, we should ask ourselves this fundamental question: "Would we agree to give up free will, and with that the ability to choose between good and bad, in exchange for a life which is peaceful and happy but devoid of freedom?" Or from random events for the sake of full predictability? To live without sorrow and pain, but without liberty, without danger and risk, but also without the satisfaction that comes with victory? To cease to live as an active, responsible person, an independent player in the universal game of life and become a passive tool in God's hand?

I am sure that only a few would agree to this exchange – perhaps nobody with the exception of some of the old, sick, and tired and a few extreme fundamentalists of one or another kind. If we had the choice of giving up free will and by so doing eliminate evil, or leaving everything as it is now but remaining free, I am quite sure that all of humanity would, in the most democratic plebiscite, vote to maintain the present status quo. We would have chosen the status that in the depth of our hearts we consider what is best to be what we already have!

In an exclusively material universe the concepts of right or wrong were absent. They appear together with life and the emergence of the soul. However, in the present, at the still initial stage of development, human beings are too overburdened by the instinct of self-preservation to comprehend truly and to apply sincerely the notion of justice and empathy. At present the basic source of evil is the lack of harmony between the strong pressure to survive and the low level of intellect and emotions. We still have too much shrewdness and too little heart and reason! This prompts the most pressing problem humanity must solve: how to endure until the proportion between these two elements will be sufficiently agreeable?

Conclusion: *The final conclusion is simple – don't demand from God more than from yourself! Be happy to live in the world which you can change into the best of all possible, God has done His part – now it is your turn!*

Summary

Reflections from above are barely a small fragment of the debate that will last for the next thousands of years, and rely on the new arguments that appear in step with the state of science and spirit of the epoch. I wish the potential members of the Affiliation of Rational Hope (if it will ever materialize) to be lucky enough to peer past even a small part of the curtain that the human race will never be able fully draw back.

Part four

Logic of growth

The following string of questions and answers illustrates the main idea of this book, namely that we live in a sensible and orderly world. In case I am not able to find an explicit answer, I give the more probable one. I would like to remind readers that this method is often applied by official science. A great part of statements of official archeology, cosmology, and biology is based on observations of phenomena which could have had causes other than those which have been chosen as the most probable.

Order

1. What is more probable – does organic life on Earth represent an order based on certain, possible to observe logical principles, or is it rather in complete chaos?

2. If it is an order, could this be merely an illusion resulting from the nature of our mind, or is it rather the real state of affairs?

3. If it is only an illusion, could the human mind create a notion of order if its own existence had not resulted from the previous presence of a larger, orderly entirety?

4. But if it is a real state of affairs resulting from a previous order, could this order be restricted to the planet Earth only? Can the Earth be the only, sole exception in complete, universal chaos, or it is rather a part of the order of the whole universe?

5. If it is a part of the order of the universe, what is this order like? Stable and unchanging, or in a state of continuous development?

6. If it is in a state of continuous development, does it proceed in a clearly visible direction or not?

7. If it does, has this direction been recognized, examined, and scientifically described?

8. If it has been, does this examination demonstrate that it is progressing from simple to complex, from dead to living, and from thoughtless to thinking?

9. If the development of the whole universe indeed proceeds in this direction, can we consider it a permanent characteristic of the universal evolution?

10. If we can, what is more likely – is this direction temporary and accidental or rather consequent and lasting from the beginning of the universe?

11. If it is steady and consequent, can we say that it reflects the nature of the entire universe?

12. If yes, what is more likely – is it result of an accident or rather of the long-lasting activity of physical laws as we know them?

13. If it is the activity of the laws of physics, what is more likely? Do these laws make a logically coordinated set, selected in such a way as to cause evolutionary order, or perhaps an accidental and chaotic collection?

14. But if they make a logically coordinated set, what is more likely – has this set been consciously designed or has it appeared accidentally? Is it possible that two consecutive, mutually complementing accidents happened – first, the accidental emergence of a coordinated set of physical laws and later the equally accidental beginning of a consequently developing universal evolution? Or is it more likely that both these events are the result of some conscious action?

15. If the second assumption is true and cosmic evolution is really an outcome of conscious design and purposeful action, can we call it a kind of consciously designed method?

16. If it is a method (or kind of technology), what is more likely – has it designed itself, quite accidentally, without any need, aim, or meaning, or was it designed by a mind conscious of its goal?

17. But if it was designed to achieve a definite aim, what is more likely? Has this aim formulated itself as a non-intentional freak of nature, or has been formulated by a the same mind?

18. If the second answer is right, can we assume that possibilities of this mind are proportional to the task accomplished – that is, designing, starting off, and supervising of the course of universal evolution?

19. If yes, what is more likely? Is this mind a non-personal, natural phenomenon, a kind of primary law of physics that exists by itself, or it belongs to some living, individual person?

20. If it belongs to a person, isn't it natural that this person possesses also such corresponding features like the ability to create new ideas, the will to act, and necessary determination, as well as all other features needed to perform such a difficult and purposeful work?

21. And if yes, can we safely conclude that the idea of the universe and method of its materialization in the form of permanent and directional evolution has been designed and realized by a living, intelligent, and motivated person?

Conclusion: *Because the existence of this person is much more probable than its non-existence, I shall consider the matter adequately demonstrated and in the further text will call it "the Absolute".*

The Absolute

22. Everything that exists materially remains in eternal, constant movement, is transient, has a beginning and an end and happens in time and space. This means that it is only a shorter or longer lasting event. This refers also to the universe, which also had its beginning and will have its end. But if this is true, what is more likely – that it is the only event of this kind in the history of eternity, or just one of many similar such events?

23. If it is one of many events, doesn't it seem obvious that the someone who is responsible for its creation cannot be subject to the common rule of transition and temporality because it had to exist before the beginning of each consecutive universe and after its disappearance. This means that the Absolute as a personification of the idea of the universal order exists always (that is, beyond the time and space) and comprises the whole spectrum of being. Not only as a person, but also as an unavoidable condition for the existence of all rationally organized reality, including the concept and performance of the truly existing universe.

24. However, as a living individual and the creator of the entire universe, He must exist also in time and space and as a living, thinking individual, conscious of His own existence, and detached from the surroundings. That is, to combine attributes which, from our point of view, seem to be incompatible.

25. What is therefore more likely? Is the Absolute a kind of an almighty, completely lonely humanlike person, living eternally in the endless emptiness of the cosmos, who in some unknown to us way is able to reconcile all these attributes? Or He is rather a being of a real, but inconceivable nature, whose existence is confirmed by the order of the universe and by our own presence here as living and thinking individuals?

26. If the second assumption is more likely, then in acknowledging the presence of the Absolute we have to agree that His true nature will remain unknown to us forever. The only way we could come nearer to an understanding of Him is to assume that between Him and us there is as much of an analogy as could be between two living, thinking beings. It is true that drawing an analogy between things known and unknown is a sin against logic, but it still gives us some hope. Because if we, like the Absolute, are alive, belong to the same reality, and have some, albeit incomparably smaller share in the spiritual world, it means that some similarities are possible. And this in turn permits us to hope that the Absolute is also in His essence both spiritual and material, but with the highest attainable share of spirituality.

27. If this is true, what is more probable? Does He use the same logic which is obligatory in our world, or perhaps some other, totally different set of notions and principles?

28. Because there is no reason to suppose a contradiction between creator and His opus we can safely assume that it is the same logic. And if this is true, what is more likely? – Did He have a definite aim in designing the universe, or has done so with no purpose?

29. But if He has done it purposefully, does the knowledge about the direction of the previous development permit us to guess what this purpose might be?

30. And if yes, does this knowledge let us think that this aim is the further, systematic increase of material complexity and spiritual growth, analogous to the one that preceded appearance of intelligent beings?

Reincarnation and responsibility

31. If this is true, what kind of development could it be? Since it will happen in the same spiritual-material reality, then it must be obligated by the same preconditions. Wouldn't a continuation of the same method therefore be the most rational? That is, a positive selection of those who show progress?

32. Since one of the subjects of this development is the intellectual-emotional entity I have called here "the earthly soul", together with corresponding physical changes, isn't it obvious that it requires a modification of the hitherto priorities that is, putting the main stress on spiritual rather than physical development? And this in turn can be achieved only by the personal effort of a person taking upon himself independent decisions in unpredictable circumstances.

33. And because the most basic features of the "earthly soul" is consciousness of its separateness and uniqueness, isn't it natural that its further development shall be individual? That hitherto development done by natural selection of the whole species shall be replaced by individual growth.

34. If yes, could it be achieved in the course of one life only?

35. But since not, does this not mean that further development of the "earthly soul" will require many consecutive reincarnations? That only the sum of sequential lives and experiences could make it more independent and better prepared to comprehend the intentions of the Absolute?

36. If yes, is it not true that a great number of consecutive incarnations would need a greater variety of environments and more opportunities for spiritual growth that could be provided by one planet only? Can we then suppose that further reincarnations may happen not only on Earth, but also in many other places within the universe?

37. If all the above is true, doesn't it mean that the general aim of the existence of the universe is the further growth of spirituality with the share and help of persons who possess a soul?

38. Since this is a process constantly realized in many other places all over the cosmos, does this not mean that we humans are only one of many examples of the universal "idea of a person possessing a soul – its version adapted to life on planet Earth?

39. Does not this mean that by playing so important a part in the cosmic theater of life, we have also become responsible for its further fate?

40. If yes, isn't it natural that the Absolute expects our cooperation in achieving the intended purpose?

41. If this is so, can we hope that that those who made peronal spiritual progress and can cope with the entrusted assignment have a better chance of transferring their souls to a following life than those who did not?

42. If yes, isn't it obvious that there must be the universal criteria of values and moral principles indispensable to maintain environment conducive to life and to the spiritual growth?

43. And if yes, this means that these values come straight out of the structure of the universe and therefore are non-relative and permanently binding.

Reality

44. But here appears the next question: why are we not able to perceive the presence of the Absolute directly? Is it due to our intrinsic inability or because He belongs to some other "super-natural" reality, inaccessible for us and governed by different logical and physical laws? To such a reality which by its very nature is inaccessible for human beings?

45. Before I try to answer this question, I have to ask what is more probable. Is there only one, single reality, common for all of us, or are there other super-natural worlds, external in relation to ours? In order to answer this question I must first make a digression to pursue the following reasoning

46. Has science ever found, in the course of exploring all accessible parts of the universe, from electrons to nebulas, any proof for the existence of any other reality placed "outside" or "above" the one we live in? Or perhaps philosophy or religion describe this kind of reality?

47. The answer is – definitely not! So far, all scientific experiments indicate that there is only one reality. The position of religion and philosophy is similar. Ancient religions as well as Christianity present "the other world" in the same convention as this one – with the same logic and realities of life. All imaginative "other worlds" are merely an improved or distorted version of the one we live in. So, we can therefore safely maintain that there is only one reality, the same for all.

48. However, another experience tells us that our life proceeds within two, qualitatively different realms of reality – material and spiritual. By the latter, I understand thoughts and emotions, abstract ideas and intellectual concepts, moral values and other immaterial phenomena. Their presence is obvious and verifiable as they are part of our everyday life.

49. Both these spheres are equally real because both give a shape to the world. Each idea must be created or comprehended by a mind belonging to someone who is alive and therefore in some way material. We don't know any idea which was discovered or invented without the participation of such a mind. At the same time observation of the material sphere of reality inspires new ideas.

50. Spirituality is a unique symptom of life, characteristic for its higher forms only. But even lifeless objects that appeared either naturally or were designed by a mind could contain spiritual values. But their potential spirituality can be discovered and activated only when it reaches a mind which is able to decipher and understand it. The text of a book written by someone possessing a soul can only be perceived by a similarly endowed person.

51. And this means that even the most extreme phenomena are neither purely spiritual or material. Each material thing is in its ultimate meaning nothing more than the realization of an immaterial idea. Since the whole universe is a realization of idea that had originated in the Absolute mind, and remains, to some degree, a spiritual event, all material things it consists of are a part of this happening.

52. If this is true, than reality is in its essence qualitatively neutral and acquires character determined by events that happen in it. Because all possible events contain specific (for them) proportions of spirit and matter, they provide analogical character to their surroundings.

53. Perception and comprehension of such reality is possible only within a range corresponding with the quality of the mind of the observer, which in turn depends on the level of his/her evolutionary development and personal qualifications. The fact that reality contains some spheres that are inaccessible to the human mind does not come from the nature of this reality, but from limitations typical for our species; although we are able to widen the range of our perception of material events by using special instruments, the way and degree of comprehending them still depends on our mental abilities. The same refers to spiritual phenomena, because we can perceive and interpret only within the range of our emotional and intellectual possibilities. The goal of consecutive incarnations is to increase the perception and understanding of spiritual phenomena.

54. If this is true, then reality is, at least theoretically, fully cognizable. There is nothing in it that by its very nature must remain unintelligible forever. Transcendence does not mean something that is beyond the boundary separating two different realities, but only what is beyond the possibility of perception and understanding of this particular individual. And this allows us to call them higher or lower.

55. We can finally respond to the question asked in point #45. Yes – the Absolute belongs to the same reality as we do. The reality that encompasses both Him as well as His creation. Nevertheless, He will forever remain unknown to us because He is far above the cognitive possibilities of our minds and senses.

Conclusion: *There is only one, shared reality that contains all material and spiritual phenomena that are possible within the perimeters of physical laws and the principles of life set by the Absolute. All that exists is happening "within" the same reality and "inside" of the same universe. If there are some other universes outside this one, their "otherness" refers only to their physical location outside "our" universe, but not to another super-natural reality. Everything that happens inside this common reality happens in time and space, has its beginning and end, and makes up always a shorter or a longer event. Everything except the Absolute.*

I hope that debate from part three of this book as well as the chain of questions and answers from above will encourage potential readers to take part in this unending discussion.

7 IV.2020

www.ingramcontent.com/pod-product-compliance
Lightning Source LLC
LaVergne TN
LVHW091313150826
845673LV00006B/1626
9798650976851